INSTRUCTION
LANGUAGE

INSTRUCTION LANGUAGE

Foundations of a Strict Science of Instruction

KARL ECKEL

German Institute for International Educational Research
and
University of Frankfurt am Main

With 65 Examples, Figures and Tables

EDUCATIONAL TECHNOLOGY PUBLICATIONS
ENGLEWOOD CLIFFS, NEW JERSEY 07632

Translated by HANS-JOACHIM SCHULZE

Title of the German edition:
"Didaktiksprache - Grundlagen einer strengen Unterrichtswissenschaft"
(Published by Böhlau Köln/Wien)

Library of Congress Cataloging-in-Publication Data

Eckel, Karl.
   [Didaktiksprache. English]
   Instruction language : foundations of a strict science of
instruction / Karl Eckel : [translated by Hans-Joachim Schulze].
      p. cm.
   Includes bibliographical references and index.
   ISBN 0-87778-257-1
   1. Programmed instruction. 2. Computer-assisted instruction.
I. Title.
LB1028.E2813 1993
510'.7'1—dc20   92-42587
                                             CIP

Printed in the United States of America.

Library of Congress Catalog Card Number:
92-42587.

International Standard Book Number:
0-87778-257-1.

First Printing: March, 1993.

The author reserves the right of
implementing the language in data processing systems.

Setting-up of the printing format with MS-WORD 5.0 and the HP-LaserJet
by RALF-UWE GLÜCK and STEPHAN BUSSE

Contents

PART ONE
Flow Logic and Elementary Representation

PART THREE

Full Didactic Representation of Instruction
Improving Readability and Testability

APPENDIX
Instrugram Examples and Description of Presentation

KARL ECKEL,

Born in 1929 in Altenstadt, Germany; studied mathematics, physics and philosophy at the universities of Mainz, Gießen and Frankfurt; taught at high schools in Frankfurt and Valencia, Spain; Ph.D. in educational research in 1973; since 1974 professor of pedagogics at the Johann-Wolfgang-Goethe University of Frankfurt am Main; Member of the German Institute for International Educational Research.

Preface to the English Edition

Instruction is the interplay of teaching and learning. The key message of this book is that it is possible to describe this interplay precisely *without saying anything about learning (the learning process) or teaching (e.g. the teaching method)*.

INSTRUCTION

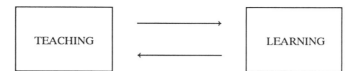

The two rectangles are black boxes which we *do not have* to know anything about. The logic of the interplay of instruction (symbolized in the above figure by the two arrows) is independent of *how* something is taught or *how* it is learned. The logic valid for *any* instruction is primary whereas methodical theories of teaching and psychological theories of learning are *secondary* because the concrete teaching and learning activities fit into the structure *provided* by instructional logic.

The assertion "Until a generally accepted learning theory is present, nothing general can be said about instruction and, in particular, no *general* structure of instruction can be found" is therefore wrong. The reverse might be true. Because of the very fact that the logic of instruction is independent of learning psychology and teaching method, *contentual* learning and teaching hypotheses may be brought into a form which may well be criticized *intersubjectively* and *empirically*. Instruction Language developed on the basis of instructional logic helps to achieve this aim.

The reason for the existence of a simple and generally valid logic of instruction is that instruction is a rather simple creation of *humanity* and, unlike e.g. learning, not a physiological *natural* process. In order to understand the logic of instruction, we need (and should) not search *in nature* but should "stick to man" and should simply realize the rules of a "game" invented by man: the interplay of instruction. That is why instructional logic, unlike the physiology of learning, belongs to the humanities! And indeed to a humanity that achieves immediate practical application by a *systematic* standardization of its terms.

Part One of the book features the strict (axiomatic) definition of *minimum instruction* and the development of its representation, using simple examples. It then shows how any kind of instruction is made up of several "minimum instructions". The structural units of an *instrugram* (an instructional script written on the basis of Instruction Language) are called *module, sequence* and *hierarchy*. The module describes minimum instruction. A sequence is a succession of modules, and a hierarchy a hierarchical order of sequences. An instructional hierarchy deals with several questions or *themes* that are interdependent from a methodical point of view: if the learner cannot cope with the initial *main theme*, he or she is referred to an "easier" theme. This procedure can be continued (with increasingly easier themes) as desired.

Part Two deals with *response judging*. It has a special position in the book in that it does not influence the definition of central concepts, which is determined by the *flow logic*. Nevertheless, attention is also paid here to the universality of concept formation. A judging structure is proposed that is supposed to contain any special forms needed in practice.

Part Three of the book aims (as is suggested in its title, "Full Didactic Representation of Instruction") at developing the systematic representation further so as to ensure the immediate and broad *practical* application of Instruction Language. Whereas Part One focuses on the *logic* of instruction, Part Three concentrates on how to *represent* instruction in order to make it as readable, criticizable and improvable as possible. Whereas the terms defined in Part One constitute the language *core*, Part Three deals with the language *shell*, which is characterized by practical aspects: the basic terms provided in the language core are used to define special terms that are appropriate for representation.

The Appendix consists exclusively of instrugram examples. It shows how to *present* instrugrams, how to incorporate into the instrugram *external* programs that cannot explicitly be described by means of Instruction Language, and finally how to incorporate *learner control*.

A glance at the detailed index makes it evident that what the book discusses is *new*.

Instruction Language has provided the conceptual base for developing a producer environment in form of a hard- and software-neutral *data base system* for the EPOS-project (European PTT Open Services) of the EC's DELTA-program (Developing European Learning through Technological Advance). There is a largely free choice of tools for the production of instruction, and "only the data formats have been laid down".[1]

---

[1] IHM (1992, p. 19). Note in particular the diagram depicted there.

The German edition has been revised and restructured to make the subdivision into *instructional logic* (Chapters I and II), *response judging* (Chapter III), *representation* (Chapters IV and V) and *presentation* (Appendix) more evident. For example, the extension of the notion of sequence, which in the German edition came at the end of Chapter IV, is now in Chapter II. Other rearrangements include the default presentation and the plain-text convention, now to be found in Point 7 of Appendix A and in Chapter III respectively. (The collection of quotations 'On the Poverty of the Social Sciences' has not been included in the English edition.)

Hans-Joachim Schulze translated the book into English. Draft translations were provided by Sylvia Georgi (Preface, Introduction, Chapters III and IV) and by my former student Antje Helfrich (Chapter V). Sarah Soulsby-Kempf did the copy-editing.

Ralf Gehrke and Thomas Jost have drawn my attention to a couple of errors in Chapter V of the German edition. Stephan Busse has helped with formatting and correcting the script. Again, I discussed everything important with Ralf-Uwe Glück, as I did for the German edition.

Frankfurt am Main, September 1992   KARL ECKEL

Preface to the German Edition

The immediate aim of Instruction Language is a clear-cut written represent-ation of preconceived instruction. Clear-cut implies that the *instructional script* written on the basis of Instruction Language, from now on referred to as *instrugram*, is unequivocal as well as fully readable, criticizable and improv-able. This is possible since *instruction is very simple in its core*. From this sim-plicity springs the transparency of Instruction Language. Transparency is es-sential to the clearness of instructional description but certainly not sufficient. The simplicity of the *basic* language has to be matched by the distinctness of representation.

Instruction Language is based on the understanding of instruction as a mere *alternating sequence of teaching and learning activities*. These are the two elementary notions everything else is built upon. Nothing needs to be said about the character and content of these activities. That is why Instruction Language can claim universal applicability and significance. Whether the act-ivity to be filled with content by the author of instruction is "good" or "bad", whether the activity is to be performed verbally, visually, or acoustically, by means of an experiment or a simulation, by means of chalk and blackboard or by computer assistance, whether it is based on behavioristic theory or cog-nitive psychology, it is always simply a matter of special cases of one and the same universal instructional algorithm. Preparing a specific lesson, the author's task remains to determine how the teaching and learning activities are to succeed each other.

The content neutrality of Instruction Language ensures not only universal applicability, but also the essential independence from pseudo-pedagogical fads and fashions, from psycho-pedagogical learning and teaching theories as well as from technological innovations (e.g. instructional media). Such devel-opments and innovations are reflected only in the *shell* of Instruction Lan-guage and do not concern its basic *core*.

The choice of terms, their representational form and the *characterization of their interrelationship* is made according to the main aim of Instruction Lan-guage: to produce a written representation of instruction that can be easily understood by instructors. This is accomplished, among other things, in accor-dance with the principles of a conservative approach towards terminology and of minimization of representation. The former implies coining as few new terms as possible, using current expressions instead. Instruction Language aims at the highest degree of congruence between how it uses terms within its own context and the conventional meaning of these terms. (Thus, what is new is not essentially new but something previously known that has been made more precise.) Minimization of representation uses definition as its most effective tool. Definition substitutes the short for the long. Recurring procedures typical of instruction that can be expressed by the core language only in a long-winded way are given short names representing *instructional types*. (These names will be noted down at the beginning of the respective instruction unit.) The more extensive the expressional potential of the language, more exactly, of the language *shell*, the more to-the-point a given instrugram can be represented.

In order to apply the instructional types to procedures that are only in part typical, we follow a kind of competitive principle: the instructional type is applicable only to the degree that it is not modified by the core language. This principle maximizes the significance of concise descriptive means and minimizes the overall representation effort. Almost the same is true for the concurrence of general and individual rules for response judging. For instance, universally applicable prescriptions are mentioned only once, usually in the lead-in to the *instrugram*, whereas exceptions are mentioned on the spot. Topographical characterization defines meaning by the specific location of the respective phrases being used. Phrases can be placed not only below each other but also side by side, so that the two-dimensional nature of paper can be fully exploited. Explicit positional relations replace complicated encodings.

Instruction Language is an appropriate means of *teacher training* since the instrugram, being both clear and comprehensive, can be examined and improved in the minutest detail. On the one hand this holds true for the command and the correctness of the subject matter, on the other hand for pedagogical and methodical aspects (such as formulation of a question, response judging, memory aids) and, in particular, for the "explanatory competence" of the *instrugrammer*: the instrugram reveals whether its author is able to give explanations; the revision and improvement of the instrugram provides information as to whether the instrugrammer is capable of learning from his or her own mistakes.

Instruction Language, however, is not only a technical language for instructors, teachers and future pedagogues. It is also a means of communication with the machine: because of its clearness the instrugram can be fed straight into the computer; it is both *script* and *program*. Consequently, the limitations of simplifying authoring systems as well as the strenuous encoding efforts of authoring languages can be avoided in the future. Costs for the development of high-quality computer-based instruction (CBI) will go down sharply because the representation of instruction by means of Instruction Language meets the demands of both person-to-person and person-to-machine communication.

The objectification of instruction based on Instruction Language will prove a useful tool in the field of *further education*, which differs from the currently existing basic education in that relatively few specialists have to translate *specialist knowledge* into a form suitable for instruction in a comparably short period of time. For them, Instruction Language will prove valuable to the development of instruction because it permits an effective and to-the-point discussion of ideas and test results; it will also prove valuable to the application of instruction because objectified instruction can be multiplied and delivered by the machine.

Since instrugrams are firstly clearly readable, criticizable and improvable by the teacher and instruction expert, secondly they can be easily fed into the computer, thirdly the computer can provide an analysis of the given lesson as required, Instruction Language fulfils the essential preconditions for a *systematic* accumulation of instructional knowledge and hence for the development of a science of instruction in the strict sense of the word. The computer can *repeat* the lesson based on the instrugram as often as desired; it can be *improved* and *tested again and again*. And all this is accomplished not under artificial lab conditions but in the "dirty" real world of field experiments. (Objectified instruction, being a commodity that can be purchased by anybody, does not depend on the institutional and organizational framework of today's schools and universities: it can stand the test of time on the free market.) Since Instruction Language provides a reliable means of communication between experts of instruction, the many diverse experiences made each day in instruction (including conventional schooling), which so far have been lost due to prevailing "speechlessness", can now be articulated and brought together in a highly competitive way. They are now participants in the striving for pedagogical truths, a process of constant verification. Individualistic impressions are replaced by simple, as it were, "socialist" facts, which in an interplay of confirmation and refutation contribute to the growth of educational knowledge. Simultaneously, the process will create new language units: interesting and successful procedures are given their own names and are incorporated into the existing body of terms (of the language shell).

The examples presented in this book have been taken mostly from student papers. They have been selected and revised purely for the reader's understanding. Their simplicity is intended to introduce the reader to Instruction Language as quickly and conveniently as possible. In addition, a practical and not too brief example has been included in Appendix A.

My colleagues, candidates for a doctor's degree and students have provided me with the necessary support to endure in the *no-man's-land* between scientific precision and pedagogical commitment. The sapling that I have planted will need their cultivation and dedication. I am grateful to them. Ralf-Uwe Glück has not only prepared the printing copy but has, in fact, looked after everything, from slips of the pen to slips of the mind. There is little in this book that I have not discussed with him. Ralf Napierski, Martin Cornel and Johannes Wagner have implemented the language in Turbo-Pascal under MS-DOS. (The translator's package consists of editor, compiler and executor.) The evaluation program developed by Napierski completes the software of Instruction Language. Kai-Uwe Beifuß, Axel Gruppe and Eberhard Palzer have helped me greatly by providing many of the examples included in this book. Large sections of the book were fed into the computer by the students Ursula Wachter, Jitka Kaiml and Cornelia Klippel. Friedrich-Wilhelm Bayerer was so kind as to check the book for printer's errors. I wish to thank them all.

This book would not have been possible without the assistance and the hospitality (now continuing more than 25 years) of the German Institute for International Educational Research. In particular, I would like to thank Wolfgang Mitter, Director of the Institute and Head of its Pedagogical Department, and his predecessor Walter Schultze, as well as my colleagues Christoph Führ and Rudolf Raasch, and finally Hasso von Recum, Head of the Economic Department and previous Director of the Institute for many years. Mrs. Sigrun Dosek was so kind as to lend me the HP LaserJet as often as possible.

Frankfurt am Main, January 1989   KARL ECKEL

HERRMANN WEYL:
What is immediately experienced is *subjective* and
absolute ...; the objective world, on the other hand, ... is
relative. ... This pair of opposites, *subjective-absolute*
and *objective-relative* seems to me to contain one of the
most profound epistemological truths ... Whoever wants
the absolute must get subjectivity ... into the bargain,
and whoever longs for objectivity cannot avoid the
problem of relativism.

KARL R. POPPER:
The irrationalist who prides himself on his respect for the more
profound mysteries of the world and his understanding of them
... in fact neither respects nor understands its mysteries, but
satisfies himself with cheap rationalizations. For what is a myth
if not an attempt to rationalize the irrational? ... And the
irrationalist not only tries to rationalize what cannot be
rationalized, but he also gets the wrong end of the stick
altogether. For it is the particular, the unique and concrete
individual, which cannot be approached by rational methods,
and not the abstract universal.

ERWIN CHARGAFF:
How many books would there be if each author had
to take an oath of originality, and to be liable for it?

KARL R. POPPER:
And, indeed, our intellectual as well as our ethical education is corrupt.
It is perverted by the admiration of brilliance, of the way things are said,
which takes the place of a critical appreciation of the things that are
said. ... We are educated to act with an eye to the gallery.

INTRODUCTION

Criticizability and Objectified Instruction

In my opinion there is very little established knowledge in the field of pedagogics. In particular, no real evidence exists as to what is good or bad instruction. To my mind, one of the main reasons for this is the fact that conventional, "freely-poised" teacher-presented instruction is a unique, individual
act. Since teacher A knows little or nothing about why teacher B acts the way
he does, he can neither learn from B nor criticize, much less improve him. A
cannot build upon what B has done, therefore everybody starts from scratch.
Thus, instructional knowledge, i.e. knowledge about instruction, does not
grow.

This growth is more likely to be achieved by means of so-called objectified
instruction, the first form of which has become known as programmed instruction. It is called objectified instruction as opposed to subjective teacher-
presented instruction because both the initial question and the corresponding
question-answer-feedback cycle have been recorded in the form of a book-
program. The teaching function is laid down to the last detail and can therefore be criticized. This ensures the possibility to improve objectified instruction and therefore to build upon what has been done by others.

The essential difference between conventional and programmed instruction (book-program instruction) can be illustrated by the following figure:

Objectified Instruction

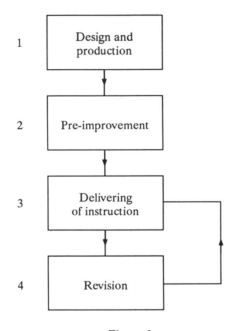

Figure 1

Phase 1, the design of the instructional script (of the book-program), can be
compared to the teacher's preparation of school lessons. However, there is
nothing in traditional instruction that corresponds to phase 2. It is possible to
pre-improve the instructional script only because it is recorded down to the
last detail. (Pre-improvement takes place before the delivering of instruction,
as can be seen from Figure 1.)
    The difference between teacher-presented and book-program instruction
that is most important in this context lies in phase 4, i.e. in the revision that
follows the presentation of instruction and the analysis of its results. Thus,
— The results of the book-program instruction are recorded in writing;
— The results can then be checked against the written book-program;
— On the basis of this comparison a direct improvement of a lesson is pos-
    sible.

The *cyclic process*

$$3 \; \rightarrow \; 4 \; \rightarrow \; 3 \; \rightarrow \; 4 \; \rightarrow \; ...$$

will lead to a systematic improvement of design 1. In teacher-presented instruction there is no such feedback: since nothing or too little has been objectified, nothing can be satisfactorily improved.

We know today that the cyclic process of book-program instruction is pure theory. The recording of instructional results is necessary for improvement but far from sufficient. In book-program instruction learners note down their (handwritten) answers on single sheets or at best in answer books. The evaluation of information thus stored is too difficult and therefore not practicable. The comparison of learner responses to only *one* question would involve too much effort. In order to deal with the instructional results effectively, they have to be stored in a form that allows any enumerations, listings, comparisons etc. to be made efficiently.[1] For the very reason that no reliable instructional theory exists, pre-simplifications cannot be permitted. If one wants to know why a question has been, say, too difficult or too easy, it must always be possible to refer back to the original data, i.e. to the answers themselves. The question is how anyone could look through hundreds or indeed thousands of answer books and critically analyze them. That simply cannot be done! Improvement in principle is one thing, actual improvement another. Book-program instruction is *weak as regards improvement*.

A second factor is responsible for the failure of book-program instruction: individual instruction geared to the needs of *different* learners cannot satisfactorily be realized by the medium book. Even if instruction was developed for one single learner, it would still have to be adaptive. *Since we do not know enough*, i.e. do not know *the* right way of instruction, any programmed textbook would have to offer a whole spectrum of instructional possibilities. (In conventional instruction the teacher reacts spontaneously to the events in the classroom, in particular to those unforeseen.) The branching needed for an adaptive type of instruction would make the book-program too complex. Furthermore, since the medium *book* cannot *process* information, everything would have to be presented in an explicit, non-coded way in the text; this would make the book too bulky, and skimming through the book would seem demoralizing. The *script* book-program is not suitable for the representation of instruction as a whole, and the *medium* book is not suitable for delivering

---

[1] All this is accomplished by the evaluation program that is part of the software based on Instruction Language.

interactive and adaptive instruction.[1] Programmed instruction is not only *weak in improvement* but also in *representation* and *delivery*.

Computer-Based Instruction (CBI)

By using the computer a considerable improvement of objectified instruction can be achieved both with regard to the impartment of the subject-matter and to the realizability of testing. Instruction delivered by the computer can be thoroughly tested. Aided by suitable evaluation programs, the author, critic or improver can display or print the response behavior as seems appropriate: either arranged according to certain learner-characteristics, according to questions or in the latter according to particular response categories, e.g. one question with all its unexpected responses from all learners. It is also possible to make a list of those questions which were not answered correctly the first time but only on the second or third attempt. The evaluation programs of computerized instructional management ensure that the author can conveniently study anything that is of interest to him. Since the computer saves "its" instruction for recall, lists of any density can be produced: from statistic and global overall judgements down to the minutest details (e.g. the wording of a specific response of any learner to any question). The computer provides the evaluator and improver with *precisely* the information needed. The results of any computer-delivered instruction can therefore be well documented and improved not only in principle but also *de facto*.

The advantages of the medium computer, as the deliverer of instruction, in comparison with the book lie in its ability to react, and compared with human beings in its speed of reaction and control. The computer's reaction made according to its analysis of the learner response can be carried out by a suitable auxiliary medium without delay. (Think for example of audio tape, video disc etc.) The principal features of computer-based instruction are shown in Figure 2 on the next page.

The whole process[2] of computer-based instruction can be divided into two parts: development of instruction and its application in practice. The former starts with a first draft that is usually tested and improved several times. In the pre-improvement phase (which takes place before the student tryout) the

---

[1] For further reference see BORK (1984) and MERRILL (1985).

[2] Any reader interested in a more detailed description of computer-based instruction should refer to the books of STEINBERG (1984), ALESSI and TROLLIP (1985) and COLLIS (1988).

The Process of Computer-Based Instruction

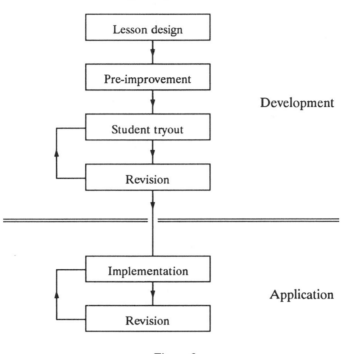

Figure 2

improver[1] will amongst other things look at the first version fed into the computer. Perhaps the screen graphics do not correspond to what he had in mind. Perhaps writing and color appear to be different on screen than on paper. Do the text and graphics match? What about the non-static and/or non-visual presentations? Do the animations, for example, proceed too slowly or too fast? What effect do the spoken passages have? Since the static-visual presentation — whether on paper or on screen — does not provide satisfactory information concerning these problems, the critic has to look at the actual instruction. For example, he will (during self-instruction) play the role of a learner, testing at the same time lesson flow and response judging. The main task of pre-improvement is the detailed preparation of the student tryout and the formulation of the "questions to nature" in such a way that one can learn as much as possible from the experiment.

---

[1] This could be the author, a member of the authorial team or anybody else.

The cycle *student tryout—revision* has to take place with a sufficient number
of learners of the same target group which the lesson has been designed for,
as many times as is necessary to release the lesson for its practical implemen-
tation with a clear conscience. A central task of the student tryout — which
as far as I know has hardly been discussed in the relevant literature — is the
mediation between the author's interest in learning and improvement and the
user's interest in acquiring reliable instruction. To make the product instruction as good as possible, the (pre-improved) lesson design should contain as
many open-ended questions as possible. The free response has to be formu-
lated by the learner himself; he can respond as he likes. In alternate-response[1] questions the learner selects from the responses given by the author.
Therefore, the author's mind cannot be subjected to investigation. The author
can learn a lot from free responses but little from multiple-choice responses.
Important as free answering may be for the optimization of the lesson, it
might also be just as dangerous when applied in "unprotected" practice.
Open-ended questions are risky. The risks of incorrect evaluation are high.
Correct responses might be graded as incorrect and vice versa and are thus
misleadingly assessed. The testing procedure should therefore start from free
questions which can be transformed into selection questions with the help of
what has been learned: the open-ended question becomes an instrument for
producing interesting multiple-choice questions.

As shown in Figure 2, application is, in our view, also experimental by
nature. The lesson will undergo further improvements throughout its practical
application. The computer makes it possible for instruction to be a constant,
purpose-oriented and constructive field experiment in "dirty" reality.[2] Research interests and practical interests become one and the same. There is a
good chance that theory-oriented experimentation or, more aptly, theorizing
restrained by practice[3] will finally replace the unconnected, side-by-side
existence of speculative theory and all sorts of fragmentary empirical experimentation that is characteristic for present-day pedagogics.

---

[1] ALESSI and TROLLIP (1985, pp. 92 and 108): "Alternate-response questions are those in which
the student chooses the correct response from a list." These include true/false-questions,
multiple-choice questions, matching questions and marking questions.

[2] I have discussed the notion of experiment in great detail in my (1978) and (1991), emphasizing
the unsuitability of laboratory experiments for the early social sciences (including pedagogics). With regard to the term *field experiment* the essential difference between the usual
activist ad hoc experiment and the − theoretically embedded − scientific experiment has
been emphasized.

[3] POPPER 1961, p. 56: "Practice is invaluable for scientific speculation, both as a spur and as a
bridle."

A Common Basis of
Person-to-Person and Person-to-Machine Communication:
the Instrugram

Present-day practice of computer-based instruction is characterized by working with *twofold* representation: script and program. The instruction expert[1] designs and produces the script or storyboard which forms the base for the programmer to develop the program that is intelligible for the computer. The storyboard is the primary representation. Unfortunately it is not unequivocal either for the programmer or for the expert critic, and therefore not suitable for intersubjective professional communication. It is only the programmer who develops an unequivocal (secondary) representation, i.e. the program. However, as a basis for communication it is absolutely useless: what is important in terms of subject-matter or instructional method disappears in the jungle of codification. Proposals for changes resulting from lesson testing or actual instruction are not put into practice because program alterations would require too much effort. Pedagogical requirements cannot be translated into reality due to (software-) technical insufficiencies.

To minimize programming work so-called *authoring systems* have been developed. These are programs which obtain through dialogue with the instruction expert the information necessary for the production of a concrete instructional program (i.e. a program of a particular lesson). The authoring systems are therefore also called *program generators*. Since these programming automatons are more readily available than (human) programmers — they are at the unlimited disposal of the author who works with an authoring system — scripts play only a minor role. The author can also do his work without them (on his personal computer). If a script is planned and used, it is not so much a prescription or description, more a sort of supplement, an ad-hoc collection of notes as memory-aids. To summarize: by using an authoring system we obtain a reduction in programming work. With regard to the demand for universal intersubjective description of instruction in the form of the primary representation, i.e. the script pattern, nothing is gained in comparison with the procedure outlined in the previous paragraph. (As for the secondary representation, i.e. the program, there is no difference whether it has been created by either a human being or an automaton in cooperation with the author. What has been said above remains valid.)

In the face of the discussed representation problem, computer-based instruction (Figure 2 on page 5) turns out to be more wishful thinking rather

---

[1] As mentioned earlier, the "instruction expert" may consist of more than one person. These people may be subject-matter experts and/or experts of methodics.

than reality. As long as there is no clear, i.e. unequivocal and transparently structured, description — a description that would permit reading, debating (the oral discussion) and severe criticism both of the lesson which has been given and the one which has still to be given — neither the development nor the application cycle of CBI will be set in motion, let alone stabilized. What we need is a description of instruction that enables *person-to-person* communication, the unequivocal, convenient and therefore binding[1] communication between instruction experts.

In order to bring about the testing and improving procedure, the representation

(i) Has to determine instruction in an unequivocal manner; and
(ii) Has to be suitable for communication between instruction experts.

If the first requirement is not fulfilled, the lesson representation cannot be made responsible for the results, whether success or failure, of the lesson. The unequivocalness is necessary but insufficient. If the representation lacks intelligibility, cooperation and criticism within professional circles, which would be necessary for a thorough improvement of the lesson, will not take place. The main point of our concern is to develop a means of representation which fulfils the requirements of (i) and (ii).[2] We call this means of representation *instrugram*.[3]

The instrugram is, in the truest sense of the word, fundamental to objectified instruction. It determines instruction, thus making it testable. It represents a specified, concrete instructional theory which can be examined in great detail in CBI. Without the instrugram, i.e. without a fixed, written pre-description of instruction, its improvement would be much more difficult. The critic could only learn something about the instruction if he took part in it himself. Even then he would only get to know one particular lesson flow. The totality of all individual possibilities of a lesson is only mapped out in the instrugram. Therefore, the instrugram is essential for objectified instruction.

If man wants to remain the master of technology or regain this mastery, he has to discipline himself, creating freedom instead of consuming it at the expense of his cultural and physical environment. This discipline also demands that the expert structures his field of activity with an appropriate language.

---

[1] The notion *binding* contains a factually hard and a psychologically mediating component: the strictness of unequivocalness has to be transmitted in a reasonable way.

[2] Both requirements are fulfilled by book-program instruction. Unfortunately, this type of instruction firstly leaves much to be desired and secondly is difficult to improve for technical reasons (see pages 2 ff.).

[3] See Preface, pages xii and xv.

Nothing more is asked for than that he should be able to communicate with his professional colleagues in a satisfactory and criticizable way. The technical language required for this also allows for the operation and command of the machine, the computer. Therefore, the problem of *person-to-machine* communication can largely be solved by making the technical languages more precise or by further developing those that are only rudimentary. Instruction Language, as developed in this book, provides an example, if not a model, for *smooth communication with the machine designed for the specific needs of human beings.* Thus, Instruction Language is under the primacy of person-to-person communication. It has been designed exclusively according to logic-of-instruction considerations without regard to the computer hardware or software.

The underlying reason for the possibility of developing an unequivocal and clear *instrugram pattern* with the help of Instruction Language lies in the fact that the cultural technique of instruction is very simple in its core:

> THE FLOW OF INSTRUCTION CAN BE REPRESENTED
> FIRSTLY IN A UNIVERSALLY VALID FORM AND SE-
> CONDLY BY USING A VERY LIMITED NUMBER OF
> BASIC NOTIONS.

Each actual flow of instruction is a special case of *one* universal flow; and each lesson instrugram is a special case of the universal and transparent instrugram pattern. Since much can be reduced to little[1] and seemingly disparate individualisms can be understood and described as special cases of something universal, the instrugram is clearly comprehensible. Its texture combines the general terms (variables) of Instruction Language such as question, response judging, feedback etc. in a universally valid way, which is the same for every lesson. What is specific about a particular lesson instrugram is nothing but the concretion of the general terms. To put it in logical jargon: *the variables and the relation between the variables always remain the same but the values of the variables may change.* For example, the instrugram pattern includes a specific, universally valid relation between the notions of response judging and feedback. In the given lesson instrugram certain *values* are assigned to these variables: it is established how and on the basis of which concrete criteria a response will be judged and it is determined which concrete comment belongs to which response.

The lesson instrugram has to reflect both the *values* of the variables and their interrelationship, i.e. the universally valid pattern of instruction. This is achieved by noting down (allocating) the values on paper or on screen in such

---

[1] Which is to my mind the main criterion of science.

a way that it can be inferred from their location to which variable they are assigned to. The placement is always the same and reflects the relationship (also always being the same) of the terms used in Instruction Language. The universally valid flow logic of instruction has been translated into a certain placement (on paper and/or on screen), which determines what we call the instrugram pattern. The respective place allocation determines the specific lesson. Since there is firstly only one placement, and since, secondly, it is a very simple one, the instrugram pattern is transparent and easily comprehensible. Instruction Language and instrugram pattern will probably solve the problem of person-to-person communication — communication between instruction experts — as far as objectified instruction is concerned.

Due to its unequivocalness and universality the instrugram can be made comprehensible for the machine — the computer — without any difficulties. The universal instrugram pattern determines an equally universal program (written in PASCAL, in C, or in any other programming language). We will call it *instruction program*. The instruction program[1] stored in the computer contains the flow logic of instruction and knows the placement on the screen corresponding to it. To transmit the data of a specific lesson instrugram to the instruction program, one simply needs to occupy the screen locations, i.e. to "write" the lesson instrugram correctly "on the screen".

The simple input of lesson instrugrams into the computer, the direct and uncomplicated way of person-to-machine communication, is largely based on the previously attained clarification of the primary person-to-person communication. This results from the analysis of the notion of instruction.

Openness

Let me finally make some remarks about the openness of Instruction Language. Instruction Language consists of a *hard core* and a *plastic shell*[2], which is able to develop and grow around this core. The hard core is determined by what is, in my opinion, true for each instruction, i.e. by what is regarded as universally valid and unalterable. The structure of the shell is moulded according to practical considerations. In practice, the basic notions provided by the language core are used for the definition of appropriate special terms. In comparison with the basic notions (such as question, response, feedback), the

---

[1] The instruction program consists of an "input-program" (editor with compiler) and an "execution-program" (executor).

[2] The language core is described in Chapters I and II, suggestions for the language shell are made in Chapters IV and V.

special terms are more empirical and more "vulnerable". What appears to one instruction expert so important that he thinks it deserves a special name might only be a matter of minor importance to another. The formation of notions and terms is the result of manifold experiences and many controversial discussions. Therefore, there is no such thing as finiteness in Instruction Language. New terms will be coined, some of which will stay, others not. Instruction Language is an open system. It is a *disciplined open system* because its terms are defined through the basic notions of the core language. Growth needs both freedom and discipline.

Basically, Instruction Language reflects a universal principle of formation of notions and language development (and also of language acquisition): vocabulary extension enables us to reduce and thereby make expression more succinct. In other words, the more (defined) words are at one's disposal, the less words are required to express a fact or situation. The special characteristic about the development of a technical language in comparison with a natural language lies in the fact that the former carefully defines its terms with the help of only very few basic terms. The technical terms are not only an indicator for the openness (of Instruction Language), they are also of central importance to the design of instruction. Without the focusing effect of these terms everything would be lost in the grey areas of the basic notions. The representation could not be deciphered. (The main aim of *definition* is not abbreviation for its own sake but improvement of communication.) Imagine, for instance, what would happen if a physicist started employing only very few basic notions, such as "mass", "length", and "time". The representation would be endless and communication would be impossible.

Part One

**FLOW LOGIC
AND
ELEMENTARY REPRESENTATION**

WHAT IS INSTRUCTION? An interplay of question and response, or, in more general terms, of teaching and learning activities. Something is explained, and the learner is asked a question. If he or she gives the *desired* answer, the lesson then continues with a "more difficult" question. But what happens if he or she fails to give the desired answer? There are essentially no more than two possibilities:

(I)   The learner is given assistance and is again asked to give the "correct" answer.

(II)   The learner is asked *another* question, an auxiliary question, which is "easier" to answer than the initial question and is connected with the latter so that "correct" answering of the auxiliary question leads to "correct" answering of the initial question.

The logical skeleton of instruction is determined by these two principles. Instruction Language is nothing but the result of the attempt to unfold the content of these principles systematically. The key statement of Instruction Language is:

> There is a universal logic of instruction. Every instruction follows the same procedure, and this procedure can be described exactly.

If this assertion seems to promise too much, I would ask the reader to consider that it says nothing about the *content* of instruction: nothing can be inferred as to whether a methodical procedure is good or bad. It does not determine empirical knowledge but ensures merely that it can be tested properly.

The terms "difficult", "simple", "right" should be regarded as *relative*, i.e. relative to the particular author of instruction; *difficult* means *difficult in the opinion of the respective author*. The terms *question, response* and *assistance* have a wide range of meanings: the learning activity *response* can in fact be a question, the teaching activity *comment* can be a response to a learner question, and *assistance* can consist in criticism.

Part One is subdivided into Chapters I and II corresponding to the two principles named above.

Chapter I

MINIMUM INSTRUCTION

Representation, Notion, and Instructional Flow

Instruction that is characterized by principle I (page 15) always revolves around *one* question. Any assistance given is supposed to lead back to this (initial) question; no new question is put but the learner is asked to answer the initial question. We call this kind of instruction that is concerned with only *one* question *minimum instruction*. Our definition starts from the presupposition that no instruction exists that does not contain a "question". Without the linking and focussing force of the question, instruction would be vague and shapeless.

In order not to overwork the term *question* we had better speak of a thematic question or shortly the *theme* of instruction. The *one* central theme may very well contain *several* or *no* questions at all (in the grammatical sense). What is decisive is the *request to answer*: a theme requires a response. The theme acts as a stimulus (that can be as little as desired). The learner is asked to respond. The answer is then judged and *commented upon* correspondingly. Whereas a *final comment* brings minimum instruction to an end, an *interim comment* requires a new answer to the question asked in the theme. Minimum instruction is characterized by the theme, the *cyclic process* "response — interim comment — response — interim comment — response ...", and by the final comment.

Flow of Minimum Instruction

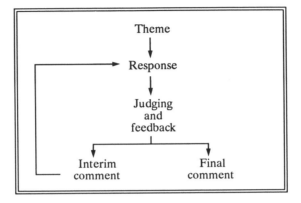

Figure 3

We call the representation or description of minimum instruction *module*. Besides the theme, the module contains the *dialogue*, i.e. the interplay of teaching and learning activities. (Theme and feedback represent the teaching activities whereas any learning activity is called response.) Using the *response keys* defined in the dialogue, the learner response is judged and commented on in the feedback. The learner is given the comment that corresponds to his answer.

OUTLINE OF CHAPTER I

The *explicit* representation of minimum instruction can be seen in § 1: the module is described in detail without the use of encodings. Neither variables, names of constants nor abbreviations are used; instead, *everything is said there and then*. The explicit representation is meant to introduce the reader into Instruction Language in a convenient way. § 2 contains the strict version of the notion *module* and the two principles that are characteristic of minimum instruction regardless of its content: the *minimal* principle and the principle of *completeness*. § 3 features the development of the didactic representation that may, in the special case, be identical with the explicit description. We will define terms that bring into focus what is essential to any instruction so as to make the instrugram[1] fulfil the requirements of good *readability, criticizability*

---

[1] See Preface, page xv.

and *improvability*. The most important concept is that of the *model comment*. It contains the aim of the respective minimum instruction, serves as a safety net for the learner and links the present module with the following one. The model comment is defined by the notions of *standard comment, model answer, addition* and *high number*.

Point 6 of § 3 (page 36) specifies the components of the *answer key* that are relevant to *response judging: name, type* and *kernel*. The key name has the indicator (the initial letter) of the *answer attribute* as its chief component:

> R: RIGHT, W: WRONG, P: PARTIALLY RIGHT, V: VAGUE,
> I: INADMISSIBLE, U: UNEXPECTED, N: NEUTRAL.

In order not to overload Chapter I, which lays the foundations of the book, we will discuss some notions that belong to minimum instruction but do not concern the instructional *flow* at a later stage.

§ 1 Explicit Representation

We will develop the essential features of the representation by using a simple example.

1. Verbal Description[1]
The following question shall be the theme of minimum instruction:

> Which city in Germany has the largest airport?

The corresponding dialogue is very simple. Only two kinds of answers will be differentiated: right and wrong answers. Instead of *kinds of answers* we will say *answer attributes*, distinguishing the R- and W-attributes of the answers given to the theme. The R-attribute will be assigned to all answers containing the expression 'Frankfurt'; any other answer will have the W-attribute assigned to it. Which comment will be given to the learner in which case? Let us decide on the following: an R-answer, i.e. an answer containing 'Frankfurt', will be given the comment:

> Right. The largest German airport is in Frankfurt am Main.

Since the lesson is finished after this comment, it will be called *final comment*, or more precisely R-final comment because it follows an R-answer. Any *first* W-answer will receive the W-*interim comment*:

---

[1] We use the terminology illustrated on page 18 (especially in Figure 3).

>Unfortunately your answer is wrong. Try again.

If the learner continues to answer incorrectly, he will be given a W-final comment:

>Unfortunately your answer is wrong. The largest German airport is in Frankfurt am Main.

For the sake of completeness we explicitly mention that a R-final comment will also be given in case an initial W-answer is followed by a correct answer.

2. Development of the Representational Form

The tree diagram provides a comprehensive survey of the instructional progression:

Instructional Tree

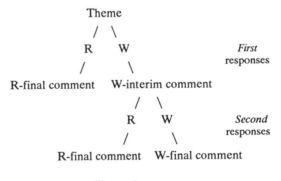

Figure 4

The flow of instruction can thus be followed in all its details. However, the tree diagram is unsuitable for the practical notation of instruction because it offers no space for writing down the comments and answer attributes. (Note that in the case of more than two answer attributes a considerable diversity of branching develops.)[1]

We will gain a form of instructional representation that works in practice on the basis of the *module flow* depicted in Figure 3 (page 18). In the first step the breakdown of *judging and feedback* represented there results in the following:

---

[1] In the case of only three answer attributes, more than ten comments would be possible.

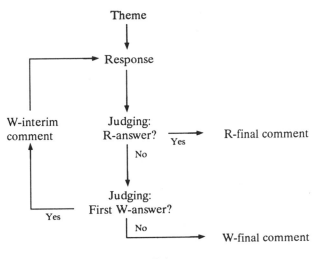

Development of Module Representation
First Step

Theme

Response

W-interim comment   Judging: R-answer?   Yes ⟶   R-final comment

No

Judging: First W-answer?

Yes   No   ⟶   W-final comment

Figure 5.1

At the beginning it is judged whether the learner's answer is a R-answer. If yes, the R-final comment is given; if no, the answer is a W-answer. It then remains to be clarified whether it is a *first* response of this kind. If yes, the learner gets the W-interim comment that asks him to answer again; if no, the W-final comment is given.

One advantage over the tree diagram is already obvious: in contrast to the tree diagram[1] in Figure 4, the R-final comment in Figure 5.1 needs to be indicated only *once*. Writing the W-interim comment on the right side results in another advantage compared to the tree diagram: *judging* and *feedback* (comments) are clearly *separated*. Judging takes place on the left, and feedback on the right.

Figure 5.2 uses flowchart symbols for *input* and *output* (parallelogram) and the diamond as the *decision symbol*. We also follow the custom of using the *lateral* outlet (of the judging diamond) for the yes-result and the *downward* outlet for the no-result:

---

[1] This is due to the explicit chronological order of the tree diagram: what happens at different times has different positions; the tree diagram provides no simplified representation for repetition.

Development of Module Representation
Second Step

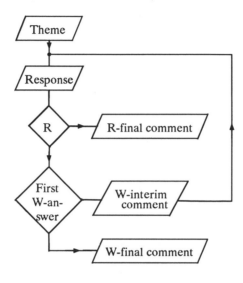

Figure 5.2

In the next step of the representational development we omit (out of Figure 5.2) everything that is superfluous, or, more carefully expressed, that can be made superfluous:

Development of Module Representation
Third Step : Topography of the Module

```
T h e m e
R   R-final comment.
W   W-interim comment.
    W-final comment.
```

Figure 5.3

The cohesion of the module that has been established in Figure 5.2 by flowcharting can be achieved without special symbols and lines: namely, by defining the meaning of the module components according to their *place* in the module in a way that preserves the coherence determined by the flow logic. In Figure 5.3 the theme comes first. It is followed by the names of the answer attributes on the left. The feedback is printed on the right: the R-

comment next to R, the W-comments next to W. The module representation
of Figure 5.2 can be reconstructed unequivocally from Figure 5.3:
— Response input takes place between theme output and response judging.
— "R-Yes" is followed by the R-final comment.
   In the case of "R-No" it is checked whether the answer is the *first* W-
   answer.
— If yes, the W-interim comment comes next, followed by the input of a new
   response.
   If no, the second W-comment, i.e. the W-final comment, is outputted.

3. Explicit Representation of an Example

If we attempt to present our example according to the structural pattern provided in Figure 5.3, we are faced with some problems. For example, shall the
(concrete) theme be labeled by the word "theme"? If not, how shall the theme
be identified? Corresponding questions apply to the identification of the interim and final comments! Finally, it has to be decided how the attribute

> the answer shall contain 'Frankfurt'

is to be noted down. The answers to these questions can be inferred from the
following form of representation:

Explicit Module Representation

01.

   Which city in Germany has the largest airport?

   R1 : 'Frankfurt'
      Right. The largest German airport is in Frankfurt am Main.
   W1
      C1 Unfortunately your answer is wrong. Try again.
      C2 Unfortunately your answer is wrong.
         The largest German airport is in Frankfurt am Main.

Example 1

HEAD and THEME:
The number 01 printed in the left margin identifies the module. The two-digit
numeral belongs to the module's *head*. What starts below the full stop of "01."
is called the module's *theme*.

DIALOGUE:
The theme is followed by name and definition of the R1-attribute:

R1: 'Frankfurt'.

(The answer attributes R, W, etc. of the module are always followed by a
postpositive digit. The reason is that *several* right attributes R1, R2, R3, ...,

several wrong attributes W1, W2, W3, ..., etc. are possible.) The R1-attribute indicates all answers that are given the R1-comment. It is determined by

: 'Frankfurt' .

The colon stands for *containing*: R1-answers have to contain the character string 'Frankfurt'. They have the following form:

... Frankfurt ...,

with the dots representing anything. Since we test the learner's answer with the character string 'Frankfurt', 'Frankfurt' is also called *judging string*.

Various comments belonging to the *same* answer attribute are labeled as

C1, C2, C3, ...

The last comment is the final comment, all others are interim comments. (If there is no C-label, the *one* comment given is the final comment.) The *sequence of these comments* constitutes the *feedback* of the respective answer attribute.

For Example 1 applies: the attribute W1, which appears *last* of all, refers to all answers that are not characterized by the attribute R1 noted *before*. In general,

(1)   The last answer attribute of a module is determined by the previous ones: the last answer attribute characterizes all the answers that do not have any of the previous attributes.

It is therefore sufficient to note down merely the name of the last answer attribute.

4. Explicit Representation of a Multiple-Choice Example

In order to familiarize ourselves with the module terminology and to lay the foundations for the general notion of the module to be discussed in § 2 (page 27), we will look at a second example (see the next page). In contrast to the first example, five answer attributes will be distinguished:

R1, W1, W2, W3 and I1.

"I" indicates the *inadmissible* answers. In our example, I1 is the only answer attribute that corresponds to more than one answer. The R- and W-attributes require (because of the equals sign) *one* particular answer, precisely one of the following letters

C, A, B, or D

and *nothing else*. If this condition is not fulfilled, the answer is inadmissible, and the learner gets an I-comment. This is a characteristic feature of alternate-response[1] modules: only those answers are admissible that comply with the *form* required in the theme. Example 1, however, is a *free-response* module: the learner can answer *freely*.

From a pedagogical point of view, Examples 1 and 2 are extremes. They are peripheral, barely realistic examples of the instructional spectrum. Example 1 is too tolerant, Example 2 too strict. Appropriate response judging usually takes place between these extremes. In Chapter III, we will familiarize ourselves with the means of producing this appropriateness: reducing either tolerance or strictness.

As for the *theme* of Example 2, we should perhaps mention that it also includes the possible answers that can be chosen. (It starts with "The metal lid" and ends with "Run cold water over the lid".)

Example 2 demonstrates that the explicit representation is inadequate: identical textual passages appear several times. For example, the R1-comment and the four C2-comments are largely identical. This representation is obviously *too* detailed. The *didactic* representation to be discussed in § 3 (pages 31 ff.) avoids this drawback.

As mentioned on the previous page, we call the comment sequence associated with one answer attribute *feedback*. Answer attribute and feedback together make up the *dialogue element*. The module of Example 2 consists of the *head* 03, the *theme* and the *dialogue*, which includes five elements, i.e. the R1-, W1-, W2-, W3- and the I1-dialogue element.

Multiple-Choice Module

03.

> The metal lid of a jam jar is difficult to unscrew. How can the jar be opened without the risk of it breaking?
> Choose one of the following answers, using its identification letter.
>
> A. Force the lid off the jar with a screwdriver.
> B. Run hot water over the jar but not over the lid.
> C. Run hot water over the lid.
> D. Run cold water over the lid.
>
> **R1** = 'C'
> Right! Hot water warms up the lid. Since it consists of metal, it will expand and can therefore be screwed off more easily.

---

[1] See note 1 on page 6.

W1 = 'A'
  C1 This method is too forceful. The jar might break.
  C2 Unfortunately your answer is wrong. The correct answer is: C.
     Hot water warms up the lid. Since it consists of metal, it will
     expand and can therefore be screwed off more easily.

W2 = 'B'
  C1 Unfortunately your answer is wrong. If hot water runs over the
     jar it will expand slightly, and the lid will not loosen. In fact, the
     opposite will happen. Besides, the jar might burst if it warms
     up.
  C2 Unfortunately your answer is wrong. The correct answer is: C.
     Hot water warms up the lid. Since it consists of metal, it will
     expand and can therefore be screwed off more easily.

W3 = 'D'
  C1 Unfortunately your answer is wrong. Cold water cools the lid.
     It will contract and it will be even more difficult to unscrew
     than before.
  C2 Unfortunately your answer is wrong. The correct answer is: C.
     Hot water warms up the lid. Since it consists of metal, it will
     expand and can therefore be screwed off more easily.

I1
  C1 Unfortunately your answer is inadmissible. It has to consist of
     just one identification letter.
  C2 Unfortunately your answer is inadmissible. The correct answer
     is: C. Hot water warms up the lid. Since it consists of metal, it
     will expand and can therefore be screwed off more easily.

Example 2

5. Historical Feedback

In Examples 1 and 2 the feedback is determined exclusively by the present response. We speak of historical feedback (and of historical answer attributes)
if the history of the answer is considered.

Historical Judging and Feedback

  01.

    Which city in Germany has the largest airport?

  R1 : 'Frankfurt'
     Very good! You've given the right answer straight off.
     The largest German airport is in Frankfurt am Main.
  W1
  C1 Unfortunately your answer is wrong. Try again.
  C2 Unfortunately your answer is wrong.
     The largest German airport is in Frankfurt am Main.
  R1 = W1R1
     Well done! Now you've come up with the right answer.
     The largest German airport is in Frankfurt am Main.

Example 3

The R1-dialogue element is a historical one (as indicated by the underlining). The R1-condition cannot be fulfilled by only *one* answer. The R1-condition refers to W1R1-answer *sequences:* the first answer must have been a W1-answer, and the second one an R1-answer.

As for the judging, the (historical) R1-attribute is tested first, although it is printed below the ("ahistorical") R1-attribute.[1] (Note that W1R1-sequences are also R1-sequences, whereas the reverse need not be true.) To sum up:

(2)   Answer-sequence attributes which are completely determined by the attribute belonging to the present answer are called *ahistorical*. Non-ahistorical attributes are called *historical*. Correspondingly, the dialogue element that belongs to a historical attribute is called historical.

§ 2 Notion and Flow of Minimum Instruction[2]

1. Notion of Minimum Instruction

a) *General Terms*

The module M is defined by its theme T and the corresponding dialogue D:

$$(3) \qquad\qquad M = (T; D)$$

The dialogue D consists of the dialogue elements

$$D_i = (A_i, F_i) \qquad\qquad i = 1, 2, ..., l$$

A_i and F_i are the i-th answer attribute and the i-th feedback of the module. As for Example 1 (page 23), the answer attributes are:

$$A_1 = R1, \ A_2 = W1.$$

The two feedbacks are:

$$F_1 = \quad R1\text{-comment}$$
$$F_2 = \left\{ \begin{array}{l} W1\text{-}C1\text{-comment} \\ W1\text{-}C2\text{-comment} \end{array} \right.$$

The number of dialogue elements is:

$$l = 2.$$

The number l stands for the number of dialogue elements in the module. At the same time, l indicates the number of the last dialogue element. In Example 2 (pages 25 f.) l equals 5:

---

[1] For reasons of readability! The historical attribute is usually (this need not always be the case) defined through the ahistorical answer attributes given *before*.

[2] This section can be omitted on first reading.

$$A_1 = \text{R1},\ A_2 = \text{W1},\ A_3 = \text{W2},\ A_4 = \text{W3 and } A_5 = \text{I1}.$$

In Example 3 (page 26) we have:

$$A_1 = \underline{\text{R1}},\ A_2 = \text{R1 and } A_3 = \text{W1}.$$

(In the abstract theoretical description the attributes are numbered *consecutively* regardless of their didactic meaning.) The full reading of (3) is:

$$M = (T; (A_1,F_1), (A_2,F_2), ..., (A_i,F_i),..., (A_l,F_l)).$$

Note that the feedbacks F_1, F_2 etc. are comment *sequences*, i.e. that feedback F_i usually contains several comments.

Arranged vertically and without parentheses, the following notation corresponds to the explicit representation:

$$
\begin{array}{ccc}
& T & \\
& A_1 & F_1 \\
& A_2 & F_2 \\
& \vdots & \vdots \\
& A_i & F_i \\
& \vdots & \vdots \\
& A_l & F_l
\end{array}
$$

(4)

b) *Formal Features (Axioms) of Minimum Instruction*

(I) *Minimal Principle*

> The dialogue of a module consists of at least two dialogue elements: $l \geq 2$.

If the dialogue contained only one dialogue element, it would make no difference which answer the learner gave. The feedback would always be the same. Obviously, that would not be instruction. The second axiom of minimum instruction, the *completeness principle*[1], reads:

(II)   Every response sequence belongs to exactly one dialogue element.

If there were response sequences that did not belong to *any* dialogue element, the instruction would be *under*-defined. What should happen if such a response sequence appeared would be uncertain. In complete contrast to this, response sequences might occur that would correspond to *several* dialogue elements: the instruction would be *over*-defined. Again it would be unclear what the reaction should be. (We should perhaps add that a *response* is a

---

[1] A set of elements is *completely* subdivided into subsets, if each element belongs to at least one subset but none to several subsets. Such a division is also called *classification* (and the subsets *classes*).

response sequence of the length 1. A response is sometimes also called an improper response sequence.[1])

A third obvious characteristic of the module should be pointed out:

(III)   A module contains no superfluous dialogue elements. For each dialogue element there is at least one possible response sequence.

This principle influences the succession of the dialogue elements in the module and thus the *order of checks* that a given response is subject to:

(5)   If an attribute A is more specific than another attribute A', firstly we have to check for A.

Otherwise the dialogue element belonging to A would indeed be superfluous. If, for instance, in Example 1 the response should not only be tested for 'Frankfurt' but also, more precisely, for 'Frankfurt am Main' (in a second dialogue element), this test would have to come *first*. If it was first tested whether the answer contained 'Frankfurt', the stricter test would be vacuous (since the character string 'Frankfurt' is contained in 'Frankfurt am Main').

2. Flow Logic of Minimum Instruction

Point 1 dealt only with the structure of the instrugram (or rather of its smallest part, the module). We will now discuss the *flow* of minimum instruction that is defined by this set-up. What has been outlined in Figure 3 shall now be discussed *in detail* and *with universal meaning*.

In order to describe the flow of instruction, we need the *answer counter* a_i: it counts the responses of the learner with the attribute A_i. To make it clear: a_1 counts the A_1-answers, a_2 the A_2-answers, a_3 the A_3-answers and so on; a_l counts the answers corresponding to the last attribute, i.e. the A_l-answers. This leads us to the flowchart on the next page.

The initial state of minimum instruction is characterized by

$$a_i = 0 \qquad\qquad i = 1,2,3,...,l.$$

No response has been given yet. If an A_i-answer is given, the value of the counter a_i is raised by 1. This is expressed in the flowchart by:

$$\boxed{a_i \Leftarrow a_i + 1}$$

---

[1] Note that three notions of response are differentiated: *response sequence, response* and *response step*. In contrast to the *response sequence* and the *response*, a *response step* is usually not given a comment (see Point 2, page 137, in Chapter V).

The rectangle is used in flowcharts as an *assignment symbol*. "$\Leftarrow$" is called *assignment arrow*, the entire contents of the rectangle *assignment* or *value assignment*. The value of the counter on the right side of the assignment arrow is increased by 1, thus becoming the *new* value of the counter a_i. At the beginning of instruction all response counters are set at zero. This *initialization* is followed by the output of the theme, the input of the response, and finally the response judging.

Flowchart of Minimum Instruction

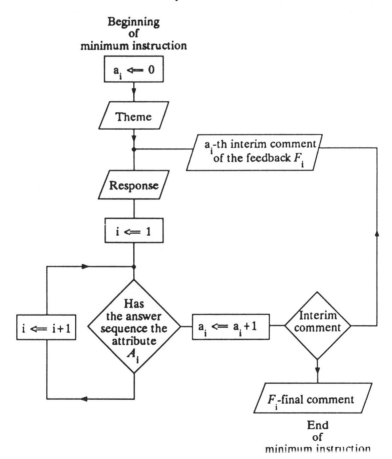

Figure 6

The response sequence[1] is first tested for the attribute A_1 (note the value assignment below the response input). If not, the attribute index is raised by 1, and the response sequence is then tested for the (next) attribute A_2, and so on. The *i-loop* is run through until the respective attribute of the response sequence is found. Rule (1) on page 24 ensures that it is found. The judging procedure implies, together with rule (1), the validity of the completeness principle (II). If the response sequence has the attribute A_i, the respective counter a_i is raised by 1. If the a_i-th comment (of the feedback F_i belonging to the attribute A_i) is an interim comment, it is outputted; the a_i-loop is run through, and a new response is inputted. If not, there is a final comment, and minimum instruction is finished.

Note: the flowchart of Figure 6 is *independent* of the representational form. The flow logic uses only the general conceptual properties of the module explained in Points 1 and 2 of this section. It applies to *all* representations, those already developed as well as those yet to be developed.

§ 3 Didactic Representation

The aim of didactic representation is to avoid special superfluous description that would reduce readability.

1. Didactic Attributes and Standard Comments
Instruction Language distinguishes seven didactic answer attributes:

(6)   **R, P, W, I, V, U, N.**

The meaning of the first six attributes of (6) can be seen in Table 1 on the next page. It presents the so-called *standard comments*, i.e. comments that are used very frequently and that are therefore predefined in Instruction Language. In the instrugram they are represented as **St.**

We already know the **R-**, **W-** and **I-**attributes. P stands for *partially correct,* V for *vague,* U for *unexpected* and N for *neutral.* P-, W-, and I-standard comments are both standard interim and standard final comments. The V- and U-standard final comments correspond to the respective first sentences of the text given in the table.

The attribute N plays a special role. We need it in order to classify learner activities which we cannot or do not want to assess. We use N, for example, in the event of *learner control,* when the learner can decide what he wants to do first and what later, i.e. when the learner can work on the instructional units

---

[1] In the case of the ahistorical judging (as in the Examples 1 and 2) instead of *response sequence* we can simply say *response.*

in the order he wants. (See Appendix C, page 172, where the menu options are indicated by N1, N2 and N3.) We also need N when the learner is allowed to answer freely and the answer is then commented upon and processed as it is (without "assessment").[1] Finally, N is needed in "reversed instruction" when the learner asks and the system (the teacher or the computer) answers. (Note that N-attributes refer to a learner control whose degree of freedom is clearly defined in the instrugram.)

Standard Comments[2]
St-*Comments*

Answer Attribute *A*	*A*-Standard Comments
R Final comment Interim comment	Right Your answer is right, but there is a better one
P	Unfortunately your answer is only partially right
W	Unfortunately your answer is wrong
I	Unfortunately your answer is inadmissible
V	Unfortunately your answer is vague. But parts of it are correct. Please answer again. Perhaps I can see whether you are right
U	Unfortunately I cannot understand you. Please try to use different expressions

Table 1

In the following example we apply the **St**-variable to the dialogue text of Example 2 (pages 25 f.):

---

[1] See Appendix C, dialogue element N_1 of subsequence [1], page 172.

[2] There is no standard comment correponding to the answer attribute N.

St-*Variable in Dialogue Text*

The metal lid of a jam jar is difficult to unscrew. How can the jar be opened without the risk of it breaking?
Choose one of the following answers, using its identification letter.

A. Force the lid off the jar with a screwdriver.
B. Run hot water over the jar but not over the lid.
C. Run hot water over the lid.
D. Run cold water over the lid.

R1 = 'C'
   St! Hot water warms up the lid. Since it consists of metal, it will expand and can therefore be screwed off more easily.
W1 = 'A'
   C1 This method is too forceful. The jar might break.
   C2 St. The correct answer is: C. Hot water warms up the lid. Since it consists of metal, it will expand and can therefore be screwed off more easily.
W2 = 'B'
   C1 St. If hot water runs over the jar it will expand slightly, and the lid will not loosen. In fact, the opposite will happen. Besides, the jar might burst if it warms up.
   C2 St. The correct answer is: C. Hot water warms up the lid. Since it consists of metal, it will expand and can therefore be screwed off more easily.
W3 = 'D'
   C1 St. Cold water cools the lid. It will contract and it will be even more difficult to unscrew than before.
   C2 St. The correct answer is: C. Hot water warms up the lid. Since it consists of metal, it will expand and can therefore be screwed off more easily.
I1
   C1 St. It has to consist of just one identification letter.
   C2 St. The correct answer is: C. Hot water warms up the lid. Since it consists of metal, it will expand and can therefore be screwed off more easily.

Example 4

2. Structure of the Module

It is an obvious disadvantage of Examples 1 to 4 that almost the same final comments have to be written down again and again. The chief aim of the present section is to introduce a more concise representation: if several final comments of minimum instruction are largely identical, they — or, more exactly, their identical parts — are recorded only *once*. This representation is linked to the general module structure of Figure 7:

General Module Structure

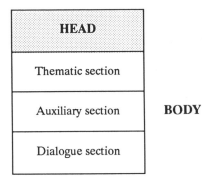

Figure 7

The auxiliary section is used for definitions that serve to shorten the dialogue. It is indicated by '**Model answer**' or '**Addition**' or, if these expressions are missing, by '**Auxiliary section**' itself.

The special case of the *explicit* representation can now be characterized as follows: the head contains *only* the module number, the auxiliary section is empty, and the theme and dialogue sections do not contain variables (like **St**).

3. Model Comment

The kind of final comments that appear in the Examples 1 to 4 are called *model comment* because they contain the *model answer*, i.e. the complete correct answer. The model answer of Example 1 is: "The largest German airport is in Frankfurt am Main." If we look at the table of standard comments, we notice that we can use the same expression for both final comments (for the R1- and W1-final comment):

<u>1</u>   **St. Model answer.**

After 'R1', **St** means 'Right'; after 'W1' it means 'Unfortunately your answer is wrong'. The expression <u>1</u> determines the model comments of Example 1. Instead of writing down this variable comment *twice* in the dialogue section, we record the model answer *once* in the auxiliary section, as shown in the concise representation on the next page.

Let us agree on the following: *The A-final comments that are missing in the dialogue section* — as compared to the explicit representation — *are the model comments;* they consist of the *A*-standard comment and the model answer according to <u>1</u>.

Concise Representation

01.

Which city in Germany has the largest airport?

Model answer:
The largest German airport is in Frankfurt am Main.

R1 : 'Frankfurt'.
W1
    St. Try again.

Example 5

4. Specific High Number
The official didactic form of representation differs only little from Example 5:

Didactic Representation
Open-Ended Response Module

01.

Which city in Germany has the largest airport?

Model answer:
The largest German airport is in Frankfurt am Main.

R1,1 : 'Frankfurt'.
W1,2
    St. Try again.

Example 6

After the name of the answer attribute follows, separated by a comma, the *specific high number* h_i. It indicates the number of comments that belong to the given feedback. In other words, the learner can give at most h_i answers of the attribute A_i

$$(7) \qquad\qquad\qquad 0 \leq a_i \leq h_i.$$

We can immediately see from the high numbers how many comments (of a feedback) are "missing" in the dialogue section. In Example 5 we started from the tacit assumption that only final comments could be omitted. (Note that a not recorded h_i has the value *infinity*: the learner is allowed to give an unlimited number of A_i-responses.)

5. Representation of Feedback
With the help of the high number, the repetition of interim comments can be easily recorded. If in Example 6, for instance, h_{W1} equaled 3, the second W1-answer would again be given the W1-interim comment. The final comment is the model comment.

In general, for a feedback F_i the following applies:

(8)   A final comment that is not specified in the dialogue section is a model comment. An interim comment that is not specified equals the interim comment given *before*.

Let $h_i = 7$, and C1, C3 and C6 of the feedback F_i be specified. Then the missing interim comments are: C2 = C1   and   C4 = C5 = C3, and the *missing* C7-comment equals the model comment.

6. Key-Related Terminology

In order to be able to express ourselves briefly and to the point, we use the terminology explained in the following figure.

Key Structure

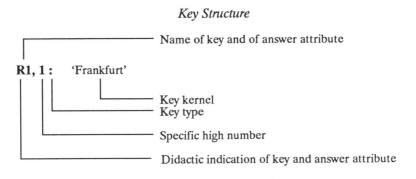

Figure 8

Figure 8 explains the meaning of the key on the basis of the R1-key of Example 6 (page 35): a *key* consists of the answer attribute, the high number, the key type and the key kernel.

There are seven didactic *dialogue attributes* (as mentioned above): R, P, W, I, V, U and N. The author of instruction (the instrugrammer) has to assign to every answer sequence one of these attributes. The purpose of this labeling is to facilitate the communication between author and reader (being both critic and improver). The reader shall be told as exactly as possible what the author had in mind while designing the dialogue. Keys with the same didactic attribute are differentiated by postpositive digits. Together, attribute indication and digit make up the key *name*. (For the sake of completeness we will remind the reader that a *missing* value of a specific high number implies that its value is infinite.)

We have so far differentiated two key *types*: the *partial type* indicated by the colon and the *equals type* as a special case of it.[1] A (not negated) *equals keys* is a strict key (and vice versa): the answer has to meet strict standards (see Example 2, pages 25 f.). Partial keys and negated *equals keys* are *tolerant* keys. They are mainly applied in open-ended question modules (Example 6 on page 35).

7. Addition and Model Comment

It is impossible to apply the simplified representation developed in Point 3 (on pages 34 f.) to Example 2. The final comment of Example 2 consists for the most part of: "Hot water warms up the lid. Since it consists of metal, it will expand and can therefore be screwed off more easily." This text is neither a standard comment nor a *model answer* (see expression $\underline{1}$ on page 34). It is rather an *explanation* of the correct answer. Such information, which is necessary for going on to the next module and which may consist in an explanation, a comment and/or in a summary, is called *addition*. Since it should be available to each learner, regardless of his learning behavior, it will be incorporated into the model comment, which consequently reads as follows:

$\underline{2}$
$$\textbf{St. Model answer}$$
$$\textbf{Addition.}$$

The exact *values* of the variable *model comment* are listed in Table 2. The expressions in bold print mark the variables to be substituted by the respective values. The final comment which depends on the respective answer can be taken from Table 1 (page 32).

Model Comment

	Tolerant R1-Key	Strict R1-Key
$A \neq R$	*A*-**St-final comment.** The correct answer is: **Model answer** **Addition**	
$h_R = 1$ $A = R$	Right! **Model answer** **Addition**	Right! **Addition**
$h_R > 1$	The answer is correct. But the following is more precise: **Model answer** **Addition**	

Table 2

---

[1] For further details see Chapter III.

The addition (if it exists) is included in the auxiliary section. *The model answer is also noted down in the auxiliary section, unless it is equal to the key kernel of the R1-key* (as in the following Example 7). In the case of tolerant judging the model answer is outputted: this is to ensure that in the possible case of a *false analysis*, i.e. if a "Right"-comment is given in spite of a wrong answer, the learner will notice that the analysis is wrong. Only in the event of a strict R1-judgement the model answer is not outputted, as it would only repeat what the learner has said before; that would be confusing.

On the basis of these arrangements we can now give a *didactic* representation of Example 2 (pages 25 f.). The *explication* of the didactic representation of Example 7, i.e. the reconstruction of Example 2 on the basis of Example 7, can be obtained as follows:

a) Since the R1-comment is not specified in the dialogue section, it is (cf. page 34) a model comment. Taking into account the appropriate key type (strict key), it reads, according to Table 2: "Right! **Addition**". If we substitute what is given in the auxiliary section for the addition, we get the same as in Example 2.

b) The comment noted down below the W1-key in Example 7 is identical with the W1-C1-comment of Example 2. Since the specific high number h_{W1} has the value 2, the missing C2-comment is a final and therefore a model comment. Since $A = W1 + R$, we can infer from Table 2:

> W1-**St**-final comment
> The correct answer is: **Model answer**
> **Addition.**

The W1-**St**-final comment reads according to Table 1 (page 32): "Unfortunately your answer is wrong." If the model answer is not given in the auxiliary section, it is identical with the R1-key kernel, i.e. 'C'. The addition can again be taken from the auxiliary section. We have now reconstructed the W1-C2-comment of Example 2. The explication of the last three dialogue elements can be obtained by analogy.

Didactic Representation
Multiple-Choice Module

03.

The metal lid of a jam jar is difficult to unscrew. How can the jar be opened without the risk of it breaking?
Choose one of the following answers, using its identification letter.

A. Force the lid off the jar with a screwdriver.
B. Run hot water over the jar but not over the lid.
C. Run hot water over the lid.
D. Run cold water over the lid.

Addition: Hot water warms up the lid. Since it consists of metal, it will expand and can therefore be screwed off more easily.

R1,1 = 'C'
W1,2 = 'A'
This method is too forceful. The jar might break.
W2,2 = 'B'
St. If hot water runs over the jar it will expand slightly, and the lid will not loosen. In fact, the opposite will happen. Besides, the jar might burst if it warms up.
W3,2 = 'D'
St. Cold water cools the lid. It will contract and it will be even more difficult to unscrew than before.
I1,2
St. It has to consist of just one identification letter.

Example 7

8. Overall High Number

The lesson described in Example 7 has a rather peculiar characteristic: the final comment is given when a learner answers the second time with the *same* letter. This will only happen by mistake, i.e. if the learner does not concentrate. We will therefore change the example to the effect that the *specific* high numbers of incorrect answers are replaced by an *overall high number* h. This means that the lesson will be finished with the fourth response at the latest. *The lesson is finished by the final comment that belongs to the respective answer attribute.* If, for example, the fourth response has the attribute W1, a W1-final comment will be given. In general: if the fourth answer is an *A*-answer, the learner is given the *A*-final comment.

Module with Overall High Number

03. **h = 4**

The metal lid of a jam jar is difficult to unscrew. How can the jar be opened without the risk of it breaking?
Choose one of the following answers, using its identification letter.

A. Force the lid off the jar with a screwdriver.
B. Run hot water over the jar but not over the lid.
C. Run hot water over the lid.
D. Run cold water over the lid.

Addition: Hot water warms up the lid. Since it consists of metal, it will expand and can therefore be screwed off more easily.

R1,1 = 'C'
W1 = 'A'
    This method is too forceful. The jar might break.
W2 = 'B'
    St. If hot water runs over the jar it will expand slightly, and
    the lid will not loosen. In fact, the opposite will happen.
    Besides, the jar might burst if it warms up.
W3 = 'D'
    St. Cold water cools the lid. It will contract and it will be even
    more difficult to unscrew than before.
I1
    St. It has to consist of just one identification letter.

Example 8

This module differs structurally from previous examples only in that the head includes the overall high number and that the positions of the specific high numbers for $A + R1$ remain vacant. The exact flow of instruction can be seen in detail in the general flowchart of minimum instruction that follows in the next section.

9. General Flow Logic

The didactic representation discussed so far should more precisely be called *elementary* didactic representation. The flow logic to be covered in the following flowchart refers to this representation. Since any *full* didactic representation of instruction has an elementary didactic equivalent, the flow logic represented here can claim universal validity.

The counter a (see Figure 9 on the next page) counts *all* answers. It is equal to the sum of values of the specific counters. It is determined as follows:

(9) $$a = a_1 + a_2 + a_3 + \ldots + a_l$$
and
(10) $$0 \leq a \leq h.$$

The check $A = A_i$ means: is the answer attribute A equal to the attribute A_i? (A is the *general* variable, and A_i the variable of the respective dialogue *element*. Compare this with the same check in Figure 6 on page 30; it is described there in words!) The main difference as compared to the flowchart of Figure 6 is that we now also check whether the overall high number h has been reached. Not only $a_i = h_i$, but also $a = h$ brings minimum instruction to an end. Note that h and h_i are *always* defined. If h_i is missing, it is infinite and has no limiting effect. In other words, if h_i is not specified, the condition $a_i < h_i$ is *always* fulfilled. However, in each and every module there is a h_i with the value 1:

$$h_{R1} = 1.$$

A *best* answer brings minimum instruction at once to an end. What happens if the overall high number h is not specified? As far as the flowchart is concerned, the check a<h becomes insignificant, since this condition is always fulfilled with an unspecified h. If the *specified* h has been defined smaller than

General Flowchart
of
Minimum Instruction

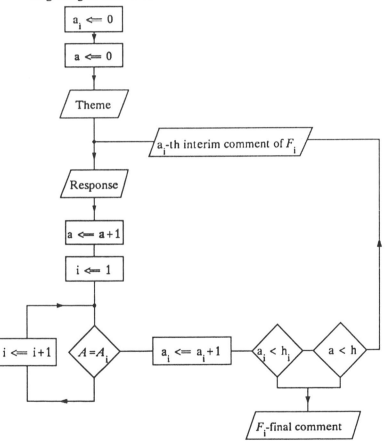

Beginning of instruction

Figure 9

the specific high number h_i, some F_i-comments, namely the last h_i-h ones, would be useless. If the overall high number is too small, these comments will be senseless. If on the other hand, the specified h was too large, i.e. larger than the right side of the following inequality (which determines the limits of the overall high number)

$$(11) \qquad h_i \le h \le 1 + \sum_{i=1}^{l} (h_i - 1),$$

the overall high number would have no limiting effect at all and would therefore be superfluous.

As for the number $|F_i|$ of the comments included in the feedback F_i, the following holds valid:

$$(12) \qquad |F_i| = \begin{cases} h_i, & \text{if } h_i \text{ is specified } (0 < h_i < \text{infinity}) \\ h, & \text{if } h_i \text{ is not specified } (0 < h \le \text{infinity}) \end{cases}$$

If neither h_i nor h are specified, the feedback F_i includes an *infinite* number of comments, "almost all" of which (all but a finite number) are identical:

$$(13) \qquad F_i = (C_i^{(1)}, C_i^{(2)}, C_i^{(3)}, ..., C_i^{(j)}, ...)$$

and

$$C_i^{(j)} = C_i^{(j+1)} = C_i^{(j+2)} = \dots .$$

10. General Concept of Minimum Instruction

Taking into account the specific and the overall high number, the equation (3) on page 27 will read as follows:

$$(14) \qquad M = (h; T; D),$$

or, more explicitly:

$$(15) \qquad M = (h; T; D_1, D_2, ..., D_i, ..., D_l),$$

with the dialogue element D_i consisting of the key K_i and the feedback F_i:

$$(16) \qquad D_i = (K_i, F_i).$$

The key K_i in turn consists of the attribute A_i and the specific high number h_i:

$$(17) \qquad K_i = (A_i, h_i).$$

Chapter II

INSTRUCTION

How is instruction made up of its *atomic* components? The simplest (almost trivial) way of putting together modules from micro to macro instruction is the sequential one: related modules that belong to *one superordinate* "theme" and follow one another in a *fixed* order, regardless of the learner's answers, constitute a *sequence*.

Sequence of Modules

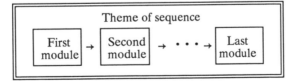

Figure 10

Since the sequence represents what belongs together in content, it acts as the minimal *content* unit, as opposed to the module which is the minimal *structure* unit. (Since a sequence may consist of any number of modules, including a single one, the notion of sequence constitutes a flexible and practical extension of the notion of module.)

A more interesting way of connecting smaller instructional units to larger
ones is *hierarchy*. According to the instructional strategy outlined on page 15,
the learner who cannot cope with the theme of minimum instruction is helped
to find the solution indirectly via an auxiliary theme. If the auxiliary theme
still proves too difficult, the learner can be assisted by an *auxiliary auxiliary*
theme (an auxiliary theme to the first auxiliary theme). This procedure can be
continued as desired. Since every theme has a corresponding module, a hierarchy of modules, or, in more general terms, a hierarchy of sequences arises.
The highest sequence is called the *main sequence*, all others (below it in hierarchy) are called *subsequences*. Whether a learner enters a subsequence, i.e.
whether or not he is given assistance, depends on his answer. The hierarchical
succession is, in contrast to that within a sequence, a conditioned one as it
depends on the answers given.

On the basis of these terms, the instrugram structure can be defined as
follows:
— An instrugram is a succession of main units;
— A main unit consists of a hierarchy of sequences. It ensures that every
  lesson is individual by keeping available the assistance needed;
— The sequence is a succession of content-related modules;[1]
— The module is the *atomic* component of instruction: parts of a module no
  longer describe instruction.

Instrugram Structure

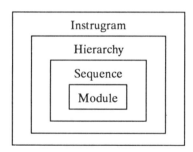

Figure 11

---

[1] § 7, Point 2 (pages 62 f.) broadens the notion of sequence to refer to a *sequence* of module
sequences.

Note that every superordinate unit need contain only *one* subordinate unit. If this is the case, we will also speak of *improper* hierarchies and *improper* sequences respectively.

§ 4 Sequence

We will illustrate the notion of sequence by the following Example 9. It shows the main sequence of an improper hierarchy labeled 021. (Hierarchy labels are three-digit numbers.) The sequence consists of the modules 01 to 04 and the *sequence theme* following the hierarchy number. In our example, the sequence theme contains the core of the question: that part of the theme that applies to all modules of the given sequence. It consists of the sequence *heading* (in our example *The Three Kinds of Triangles*), and the sequence *lead-in* (in our example the following three lines). Note that the sequence theme may consist solely of the sequence heading that serves as a point of orientation for the learner; the sequence heading is a *necessary*, and the sequence lead-in a *potential* constituent of the sequence theme. Also note that the sequence theme does not contain a request to answer; this is included in the module.

Improper Hierarchy with Proper Main Sequence

021.   *The Three Kinds of Triangles*

> We distinguish between three kinds of triangles: acute, right and obtuse triangles. What is the name of the triangle shown below? Select the correct identification letter!
>
> A. acute; B. right; C. obtuse.

01.

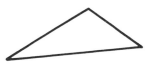

R1,1 = 'C'
   An obtuse triangle is a triangle one of whose angles is an
   obtuse angle.
W1   = 'A'
   St. An acute angle is smaller than 90 degrees.
W2   = 'B'
   St. A right angle is exactly 90 degrees.
   I 1,2
   St. It has to consist of just one identification letter.

02.

R1,1 = 'A'
An acute triangle is a triangle all of whose angles are acute.
W1 = 'B'
St. Only angles that are exactly 90 degrees are called right angles.
W2 = 'C'
St. Only angles that are larger than 90 degrees are called obtuse angles.
I 1,2
St. It has to consist of just one identification letter.

03.

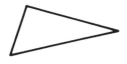

R1,1 = 'C'
W1 = 'A' v 'B'
St. Look at the largest angle.[1]
I 1,2
St. It has to consist of just one identification letter.

04.

R1,1 = 'B'
A right triangle is a triangle one of whose angles is a right angle.
W1 = 'A' v 'C'
St. Look at the largest angle.
I 1,2
St. It has to consist of just one identification letter.

Example 9

---

[1] The key **W1** = 'A' v 'B' requires: the answer has to equal 'A' *or* 'B'. The letter 'v' stands for *or*.

§ 5 Proper Hierarchy

A proper hierarchy contains at least one subsequence. The learner enters it provided that he has given a particular answer in the superordinate sequence. We will explain the instructional flow that is characterized by hierarchy on the basis of the relatively simple Example 10 (on the next page). The hierarchy 002 consists of the main sequence "Area of a Square" and the subsequence "Units of Area" indicated by

Sequence 1

or by brackets

[1]

in front of the subsequence heading.

The sequences of our example contain only one module each. The (proper) hierarchy 002 consists of an improper sequence which contains only one module. Subsequence 1 follows the C2-comment of the U-key: the learner then, and only then, enters the subsequence when he gives a U-answer for the second time. The C2-comment of the U-dialogue element is called *source comment* since the subsequence has its source there. In general:

(1)   Subsequence instruction directly follows the corresponding source comment.

The flow of instruction *within* a subsequence module does not differ from the usual intramodular flow. A final comment in the subsequence is followed by the return to the main sequence (being the superordinate sequence) or, to be more precise, the theme of the main sequence module.[1] Instruction returns from a subsequence to a source module (i.e. to the module that the source comment belongs to) as often as the high number of the source key, the *source limit*, permits. Remember the meaning of the specific (i.e. belonging to a specific answer attribute) high number. It indicates how many answers of the respective answer attribute can be given at most. As in Example 10, five U-answers may be given in the module of the main sequence. On "descending" into the subsequence, the U-counter a_U shows 2: another three U-answers may be given; the return into the main sequence is therefore possible. If h_U had the value 2, there would be no way back; the lesson would be finished with the subsequence. Note also that at the moment of the return from the subsequence, all other high numbers of the main sequence module have not been reached.

---

[1] Including the heading of the main sequence ("Area of a Square").

Proper Hierarchy with Improper Sequences

002.   *Area of a Square*

Find the area A of a square whose sides have length a.

$$A =$$

R1,1 = 'a^2'
P1,2 = '$a \cdot a$'
   St. Write your answer as a power!
W1,3 = '2a'
   C1 St. This is not a line segment but a surface!
   C2 St. If a = 3 cm, then 2a = 2·3 cm = 6 cm. The unit *cm* is a unit of length.
U ,5
   C1 St. Your answer has to be in single signs, not in words.
   C2 St.
   Sequence 1.
   C3 St. Think what characteristics a rectangle must have to be called a square. Knowing that, you will have no difficulty in finding the formula for the area of a square.
   C4 St. A square is a rectangle whose sides are all equal.

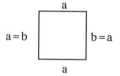

[1]   *Units of Area.*[1]

Think of the square units. Tell me some!

Model answer: km^2, m^2, cm^2 or mm^2.
Addition: Now go back to the inital question:

R1,1 :   'km^2' v 'm^2' v 'cm^2' v 'mm^2'
U ,3
       St.

Example 10

---

[1] In the subsequence [1] the **addition** serves as rhetoric leading-back to the initial question.

The return condition is (while ignoring the *overall* high number):

(2)   On finishing a subsequence, instruction is continued in the source module, provided the difference between the source limit and the specific answer counter is more than zero.

Thus, the high numbers regulate not only the intramodular but also the overall (intersequential) hierarchical flow of instruction.

Note also that if there is no source comment *recorded* in the relevant section, the learner is referred straight to the named subsequence. An unrecorded source comment never has the meaning of a model comment. (See also Chapter I, page 34, last paragraph.)

§ 6 Notion of Hierarchy

In order to become more familiar with the representation and the flow logic of the instructional hierarchy, let us take another, more complex example.

Proper Hierarchy of Depth 2

026.   *Area of a Parallelogram.*

Find the area A of the following quadrilateral! Enter the identification letter of the correct answer.

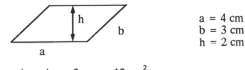

a = 4 cm
b = 3 cm
h = 2 cm

A. $A = a \cdot b = 4 \text{ cm} \cdot 3 \text{ cm} = 12 \text{ cm}^2$
B. $A = a \cdot h = 4 \text{ cm} \cdot 2 \text{ cm} = 8 \text{ cm}^2$
C. $A = (a \cdot b) : h = (4 \text{ cm} \cdot 3 \text{ cm}) : 2 \text{ cm} = 6 \text{ cm}$

Addition: As the figure is a parallelogram, the area A can be found by multiplying the length of one side with that of the corresponding altitude.

R1,1 = 'B'
W1,2 = 'A'
        St.
        Sequence 1.
W2,2 = 'C'
        St.
        Sequence 2.
    I 1,2
        St.

[1]   *Two Kinds of Quadrilaterals.*

01.

What characteristics do the following quadrilaterals have?

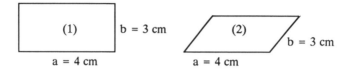

A. Opposite sides are parallel in both figures. Both quadrilaterals are therefore parallelograms with at least one right angle.
B. Diagonally opposite angles are equal in both figures. Both figures are therefore rectangles.
C. Quadrilateral (1) has four right angles and is therefore called rectangle. In quadrilateral (2) opposite sides are equal. It is therefore called parallelogram.
D. Quadrilateral (1) is straight, quadrilateral (2) is oblique. Therefore the first figure is called straight rectangle, the second one oblique rectangle.

Addition: Rectangles are special parallelograms with not only opposite sides being equal but also all angles being right angles.

R1,1 = 'C'
W1,2 = 'A'
        St. True, opposite sides are parallel, but whereas quadrilateral (1) has four right angles. quadrilateral (2) has none!
W2,2 = 'B' v 'D'
        St. The word *rectangle* indicates that the figure has to have right angles.
   I 1,2
        St.

02.

On the left, we have a *special* parallelogram, i.e. a rectangle, and on the right we have a parallelogram *without right angles*.

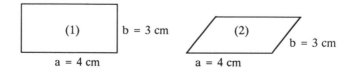

A. The areas are the same since both pairs of opposite sides are equal.
B. The area of (2) is smaller since the parallelogram has a shorter altitude.
C. The areas of the two quadrilaterals cannot be compared.
D. The areas are not the same because the quadrilaterals are not congruent.

Select the identification letter of the correct answer.

Addition: The area of the parallelogram can be found on the basis of that of the rectangle. If you want to find the area of a parallelogram, you have to start from two lines that are perpendicular to each other.

R1,1 = 'B'
W1,2 = 'A'
    St. Note that figure (2) has no right angles!
W2,2 = 'C' v 'D'
    St. The area of a parallelogram can be found by converting it into a rectangle of the same area.
I 1,2
    St.

[2]   *Area of a Rectangle.*

01.

Which units of measurement can be used to refer to the area of a quadrilateral? Choose the identification letter of the correct answer.

A. The area of a figure measures its perimeter, using the units mm, cm, dm, m, etc.
B. The area of a figure measures its surface, using the units mm^2, cm^2, dm^2, m^2, etc.
C. The area of a figure also depends on the surrounding space. Its units are mm^3, cm^3, dm^3, m^3, etc.

R1,1 = 'B'
W1,2 = 'A' v 'C'
    St.
I 1,2
    St.

02.

Find the area A of the following rectangle:

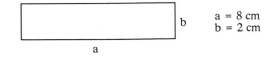

a = 8 cm
b = 2 cm

A. $A = a \cdot b = 8 \text{ cm} \cdot 2 \text{ cm} = 16 \text{ cm}^2$
B. $A = a + b = 8 \text{ cm} + 2 \text{ cm} = 10 \text{ cm}$
C. $A = a \cdot (a + b) = 8 \text{ cm} \cdot (8 \text{ cm} + 2 \text{ cm}) = 80 \text{ cm}^2$

R1,1 = 'A'
W1,2 = 'B' v 'C'
    St.
    Sequence 21.
  I 1,2
    St.

[21]   *How to Find the Area of a Rectangle*

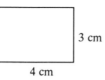

3 cm

4 cm

Imagine dividing up the surface of a rectangle into squares of 1 cm in length. How many squares do you get?

A. 7
B. 12
C. I don't understand the question.

Choose one identification letter.

Addition: The following figure shows the division of the rectangle into squares of the side 1 cm:

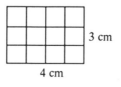

3 cm

4 cm

Thus, the rectangle consists of
    four times three
squares. You multiply the number of units in the length by the number of units in the width:

$$A = 4 \text{ cm} \cdot 3\text{cm}$$
$$= 4 \cdot 3 \cdot \text{cm} \cdot \text{cm}$$
$$= 4 \cdot 3 \cdot \text{cm}^2$$
$$= 12 \text{ cm}^2$$

Of course you can also start:
$$3 \text{ cm} \cdot 4 \text{ cm}.$$

The result is the same.

R1,1 = 'B'
    St.
W1,2 = 'A'
    St. Either you simply added both sides, or you counted
    incorrectly.
W2,2 = 'C'
    I will help you. We will solve a similar problem together. If
    you divide up a rectangle 5 cm long and 4 cm wide into
    squares of the side 1 cm, you get the following figure.

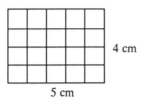

    The rectangle therefore contains
              five times four
    squares; the area is 20 cm^2. Now go back to the initial
    question.
I 1,2
    St.

Example 11

1. Labels

Hierarchy 026 contains four sequences: the main sequence 026, its two subsequences [1] and [2], and the (sub-)subsequence [21] belonging to [2].

In general: the main sequence has the same label as the hierarchy it belongs to. All other sequences are indicated by brackets. The subsequences of the main sequence are: [1], [2], [3], ..., [9]. (We assume that any sequence can have at most 9 subsequences.[1]) The sequences of depth 2 are labeled as follows:

$$[11], ..., [19]; ...; [91], ..., [99].$$

The first figure indicates the origin, i.e. the "parent sequence", the second one the number of the subsequence.

---

[1] Because of notational simplicity. In case of more than 9 subsequences, say 20, we have to separate the labels by a special sign, say, a semicolon. The sequences of depth 2 would then be labeled as: [1;1], ..., [20;20].

General Hierarchy of Sequences

	Main sequence			d = 0
[1]	[2] ...	[9]		d = 1
[11]...[19]	[21]...[29]	...	[91]...[99]	d = 2
[111]...[119]		...	[991]...[999]	d = 3
.	.		.	.
.	.		.	.
.	.		.	.

Figure 12

In Example 11 the subsequence 21 originates from the parent sequence 2. The concrete labels for this example are provided in the following table:

Labeling of Sequences and Modules

Label within the Instrugram	Context-Independent Label
026	{ Hierarchy 26 / Main sequence 26
[1] *or* Sequence 1	Sequence 26.1
[2] *or* Sequence 2	Sequence 26.2
01	Module 26.2;1
02	Module 26.2;2
[21] *or* Sequence 21	Sequence 26.21

Table 3

The sequences of depth d (d>0) in a given hierarchy are indicated by d-digit numbers, in particular by

$$\text{sequence } s_1 s_2 s_3 ... s_d,$$

(3) in the source module, and by brackets

$$[s_1 s_2 s_3 ... s_d]$$

before the sequence heading.

The position of sequences in the hierarchical representation depends on the numerical value of the labels. A smaller value implies an earlier position: [1], ..., [9]; [11], ..., [99]; [111], ..., [999]; ... .

The *full*, context-*independent* labeling of a sequence of depth d reads:

$$s_0.s_1s_2...s_d,$$

with s_0 being the label of the hierarchy or main sequence. The full, context-independent label of a *module* m_d reads:

$$s_0.s_1s_2...s_d; m_d.$$

2. Hierarchy Diagram

The following figure serves to clarify the structure of hierarchy applied to our example. The (double-framed) outer rectangles represent the sequences, the (single-framed) inner ones stand for the modules.

Hierarchy Diagram

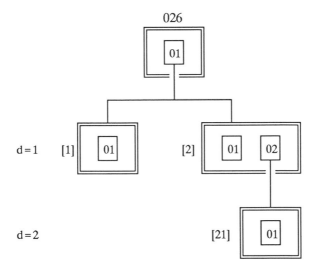

Figure 13

The above representation can be generalized as desired. This applies both to the number of sequences with a given depth and to the depth itself.

3. Instructional Flow in a Hierarchy

Let us now complete our hierarchy illustration by making fully visible the instructional flow between the sequences and between the modules of the hierarchy. Figure 14 depicts the intermodular flow of Example 11 in an unequivocal way, except for the number of runs through the loops, which is determined by the respective source limits.

Hierarchical Flow

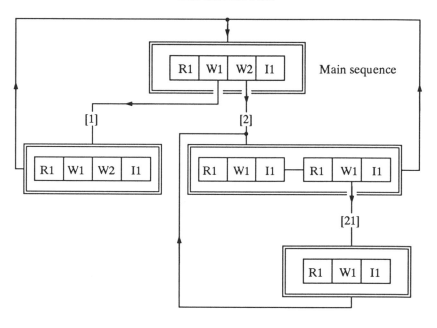

Figure 14

The lesson starts with the main sequence, which consists of only one module. Only W1- or W2- answers are relevant for the intermodular flow, since only the first W1- and the first W2-comment are source comments. After the first W1-answer the lesson continues in the first auxiliary subsequence. After finishing the subsequence, i.e. after a final comment, the learner returns to the main sequence. The reason is that the relevant source limit (the W1-high number of the main sequence) equals 2. By the same token, there is no second "descent" into [1], since in the case of a second W1-answer, the high number 2 must lead to the W1-final comment (in the main sequence).

In the case of a W2-answer (in the initial sequence) the learner is passed on into the second subsequence of the depth 1, i.e. into [2], namely to its first module 01.

If in the module 02 of sequence [2] the learner gives a W1-answer, the lesson continues with the lowest subsequence [21]. Having finished the lowest subsequence, the lesson returns to source module 01 of sequence [2], because the high number of the (W1-) source comment is larger than 1. Again, there is exactly one return (high number equals 2).

In the case of a second W1-answer in this module, there is *no* second branching into [21] because of $h_{w1} = 2$. Instead, the learner is given a final comment, and the next module of the same sequence, i.e. 02, follows. (As the modules follow one another immediately, so does instruction, *provided there are no subsequences*.) On finishing the subsequence [2] the lesson returns to the main sequence, since the source limit of the W2-key in the main sequence equals 2.

Each of the flow lines is run through once at most, since all source limits equal 2. In general: a subsequence is run through as often as the (source) comment it belongs to.[1]

4. Table of Contents (Sequence Headings)
Every sequence heading has a learner-oriented content component printed in italics.[2] The total of these components makes up the hierarchy-related table of contents suited to the learner. In our example it is as follows:

Table 4

The table of contents of an *instrugram* (being a succession of hierarchies) provides a good overall view of what can be learnt in the respective lesson. It

---

[1] In the event of C-labeling the following applies: an interim comment $C^{(j)}$ is run through (j'-j) times at most, with $C_i^{(j')}$ being the next comment recorded after $C_i^{(j)}$. (See also page 42.)

[2] The sequence heading is the minimum component of the sequence theme (see page 45).

increases the criticizability of the instrugram because it can now be tested whether the instrugram keeps what is promised in the detailed table of contents.

Besides the learner-oriented information printed in italics, the *full* table includes *optional* methodical hints in roman type that are designed *exclusively* for the teacher or trainer and critic of instruction and that do not appear in the lesson. (See also the table of headings in Appendix A on page 152.) The instructional expert is informed in conventional metalanguage on both the methodical role and the content of the sequences, the learner only on the latter. (The sequence heading has nothing to do with the flow logic!)

5. Final Comment as Source Comment

If a subsequence is designed so that correct answering of the subtheme includes the required answer to the source theme, the return to the source module would be useless. This happens in Example 12. The lesson finishes in the subsequence. The return to the parent sequence is prevented by the C2-source comment's being the *final comment*. With the W1-answer the learner has already used up the number of (wrong) answers he was allowed to give; the source limit 2 has been reached by the time that instruction in the subsequence starts. (See also expression (2) on page 49.)

Example of a One-Way Hierarchy

001.   *Formula for the Area of a Rectangle.*

How do you find the area of a rectangle?

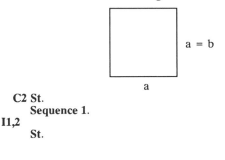

R1,1 = 'a·b'
       St. The area of a rectangle is found by multiplying two adjacent sides.
W1,2 = 'a^2'
       C1 St. In this case the rectangle would look like this:

a = b

a

       C2 St.
           Sequence 1.
   I1,2
           St.

[1]   *Rectangle with Given Side Lengths and Given Area.*

An illustrative example: side x is 5 cm, side y is 3 cm. The area of this rectangle is 15 cm^2.

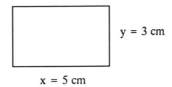

y = 3 cm

x = 5 cm

How do you think this result is calculated? Answer by entering a mathematical or arithmetical expression.

Addition: The area of a rectangle is found by multiplying two adjacent sides.

R1,1 = 'x·y' v '3 cm·5 cm'
W1,3
   St.

Example 12

The following figure shows the flow of the preceding example:

*Instructional Flow in a
One-Way Hierarchy*

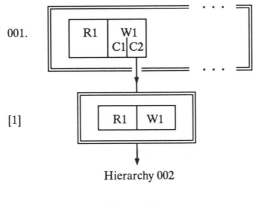

001.

[1]

Hierarchy 002

Figure 15

Having finished the assistance instruction, the learner does not return to the main sequence but begins with the instruction of the next hierarchy.

§ 7 General Flow of Instruction and Repetition of Instrugram Parts

Let us first discuss the generalization of the instructional flow for *any number of* modules, sequences and hierarchies. In Point 2 we will add a last concept to the *core* of Instruction Language, the notion of *structured sequence*, in order to be able to represent the *succession* of sequences.[1] This should make our language system complete with respect to the flow logic. Finally, we will discuss in Points 3 and 4 how the repetition of hierarchies and that of well-defined parts of hierarchies is written down.

1. Instructional Flow in Simple Sequences

Preliminary remark: the adjective *simple* in the heading indicates that the instructional flow to be discussed here is not the general one. Simple sequences are nothing but sequences of the kind we have dealt with until now. (The generalization into *structured* sequences is to follow in Point 2.)

The instructional flow determined by the instrugram pattern is represented in Figure 16 on the next page. It starts with the main sequence of the first hierarchy, or, to be more precise, with the sequence theme (which contains no "effective" question). It is followed by the first module of the sequence, whose instruction is analyzed in the inmost frame of the flow illustration. (The addition "as yet unfinished" refers to the number of return runs to be discussed below.) Let us now take a closer look at the most inward frame. It is first determined whether a source comment belongs to the given response. If this is not the case, we speak of a *conservative* comment. If the conservative comment is a final comment, two cases need to be differentiated: a) if the learner is *not* in a final module of a sequence, the lesson continues in the next module; b) if the learner *is* in the final module of a sequence, and *if there is no possibility of return within the hierarchy,* the hierarchy instruction is finished. Instruction is either continued in the following hierarchy, or we are at the end of the instrugram. (Note that in this context "following" can mean either *following immediately* or *later on.* In the latter case, instruction jumps to the hierarchy indicated by a specific *address,* e.g. 'Go to 020'.)

When does instruction return to a sequence that is superior in hierarchy? Whenever at least one of the source comments that the given sequence descends from either directly or indirectly belongs to a non-final module of the respective source sequence and/or is an interim comment of the source

---

[1] Note that the succession of modules is represented as a *sequence* and that of hierarchies as an *instrugram* (or part of an instrugram).

Flow of Instruction

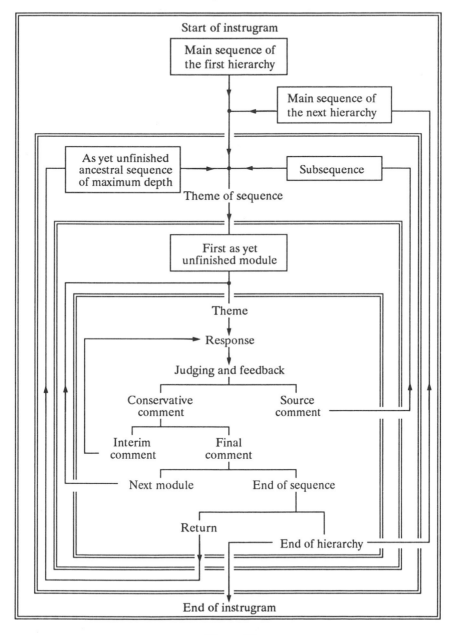

Figure 16

sequence. Such a sequence may be referred to *as yet unfinished ancestral sequence*.[1] If there are several such sequences, instruction returns to the ancestral sequence that is next to it (the ancestral sequence of *maximum depth*.)

Note further that after a source comment the lesson continues in the corresponding subsequence.[2]

2. General Instructional Flow and Structured Sequences

The structured sequence is essentially a sequence of module sequences. The structured sequence is also called *full sequence* and the unstructured sequences included in it *part-sequences*.

Set-Up of the Structured Sequence

Full-sequence head

Part-sequence theme
01.
02.
.
.
.

Part-sequence theme
01.
02.
.
.
.

Part-sequence theme
01.
02.
.
.
.

.
.
.

Figure 17

Since only *full* sequences can be subsequences, the *hierarchy of instructional flow* according to Figure 16 (page 61) remains valid. Only the intrasequential flow changes slightly: in Figure 18 (next page), by contrast to Figure 16, it is asked at the end of a sequence whether a *full* sequence or a part-sequence has been finished, i.e. whether a *structured* sequence has been finished com-

---

[1] Instruction returns to the source sequence until all modules of the subsequence are run through. A sequence is either run through fully or not at all.

[2] In terms of content, subsequences need not be assistance sequences. They can also be critical in character, if for example an explanation is asked after a *correct* answer has been given.

pletely or partly. (The terms 'full sequence' and 'structured sequence' are synonyms.)

Universal Intrasequential Instructional Flow
Modification of Figure 16

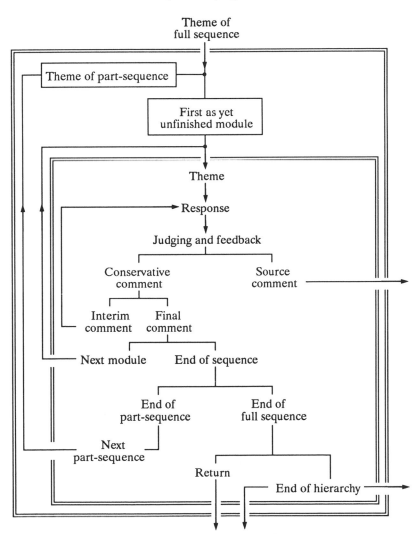

Figure 18

3. Repetition of Sequences

First an example:

Repetition of Sequences

001.   *The Second Binomial Formula.*

What is $(a-b)^2$?

Enter the identification letter of the correct answer.

A. $a^2 + b^2$.
    Reason: the exponent 2 behind the parentheses becomes the
    exponent 2 of the numbers in parentheses. The following rule
    applies: the square of a difference is equal to the sum of
    squares a^2 and b^2.

B. $a^2 + 2ab + b^2$.

C. $a^2 - b^2$.
    Reason: the exponent 2 behind the parentheses becomes the
    exponent 2 of the numbers in parentheses. The following rule
    applies: the square of a difference is equal to the difference of
    squares a^2 and b^2.

D. $a^2 + 2ab - b^2$.

E. $a^2 - 2ab + b^2$.

F. $a^2 - 2ab - b^2$.

R1,1 = 'E'
W1,2 = 'A'
    St. Apparently, you do not remember how to add negative
    numbers. We will discuss that again.
    Sequence 1.
W2,2 = 'F'
    St. Apparently, you do not remember exactly how to multiply
    negative numbers. We will discuss that again.
    Sequence 2.
W3,2 = 'D'
    St. Calculating with negative numbers seems to be difficult
    for you. I will help you:
        CALCULATING WITH NEGATIVE NUMBERS
    Sequence 1/2.
W4,2 = 'A' v 'C'
    St. Squaring binomials is not that easy. $(a-b)^2$ means to
    multiply (a-b) by itself, i.e. (a-b)(a-b). Multiply *every* term of
    one difference with *every* term of the other.
I 1,2
    St.

[1] *Addition of Negative Numbers*

01.

Calculate -3 -2 .

R1,1 = '-5'
W1,2 = '5'
> St. The two negative numbers -3 and -2 have to be added.
> Written in full, the exercise reads
> $$(-3) + (-2).$$
> If you go three steps to the left and then another two to the left, that makes five steps to the *left* but not five steps to the *right*.

W2,2 = '-1'
> St. You subtracted 2 from 3, which makes 1, and prefixed the minus sign (belonging to the number 3) to the result, which makes it -1. However, that would be another exercise, namely
> $$-(3 - 2).$$
> If you remove the parentheses you get
> $$-3 + 2.$$
> The exercise that you are supposed to do reads in full
> $$(-3) + (-2).$$
> If you borrowed $ 3 and then another $ 2, you would have borrowed $ 5 and not just $ 1.

U ,1
> St. This is how to find the right result:
> $$-3 - 2 = (-3) + (-2)$$
> $$= -5.$$

02.

Calculate -x - x .

R1,1 = '-2x'
W1,2 = '0'
> St. You calculated - (x - x), which in fact makes zero.
> However, you are supposed to calculate (-x) + (-x).

W2,2 = '2x'
> St. Maybe you are thinking of the rule:
> $$\text{MINUS TIMES MINUS GIVES PLUS.}$$
> However, this is not a multiplication but an addition as you will notice if you write out the exercise in full, i.e.:
> $$(-x) + (-x).$$

U ,1
> St. Calculate like this:
> $$-x - x = (-x) + (-x)$$
> $$= -2x.$$

[2]   *Multiplication of Negative Numbers*

What is   -2·(x - 4)?

R1,1 = '-2x + 8' **v** '8 - 2x'
W1,2 = '-2x - 8'
    St. If two negative numbers are multiplied, the result is a
    positive number.
U ,2
  C1 St.
  C2 St. This is how the calculation works:
$$-2·(x - 4) = -2x + (-2)·(-4)$$
$$= -2x + 8.$$

Example 13

Example 13 has a new term,

<u>1</u>   Sequence 1/2,

in the W3-dialogue element of the main sequence. The expression <u>1</u> has the
effect that after the F3-source comment *firstly the instruction according to
sequence* [1] *occurs and immediately afterwards the instruction according to
sequence* [2]. Thus, <u>1</u> determines a repetition of instruction which has already
been determined elsewhere (for different purposes). The *two unstructured*
sequences [1] and [2] form, as determined by <u>1</u>, *one structured* sequence.

4. Repetition of Hierarchies and Parts of Hierarchies
Using the notion of subsequence and that of part-sequence, the repetition of
hierarchies (and parts of hierarchies) can be defined.

Diagram: Hierarchy Repetition

001.
    . . .
002.
    . . .
003.
   . . .
    Hierarchy 1/2.
004.
    . . .

Figure 19

Hierarchies 001 and 002 together form *one* subsequence of hierarchy 003.
Under special circumstances (not to be specified here), the hierarchies 001

and 002 are repeated *subsequently* in the course of the 003-instruction: the *succession* of the hierarchies 001 and 002 *in the hierarchy 003* functions as (one) subsequence. Taken on their own, 001 and 002 form *part*-sequences of this subsequence.[1] (The return of instruction from this structured subsequence to the higher sequences of 003 and/or the progression to hierarchy 004 take place according to the general rules discussed in Point 1 starting from page 60.)

The generalization of the repetition expression

$\underline{2}$ Hierarchy 1/2

is obvious:

$\underline{3}$ Hierarchy $j_1/j_2/.../j_n$.

If the *labels* $j_1, j_2, ..., j_n$ follow each other immediately in order of size, i. e. if each successor is greater than its predecessor by 1, then instead of $\underline{3}$ we write:

$\underline{4}$ Hierarchy $j_1 - j_n$.

One final generalization: naturally, meaningful *parts* of hierarchies can be repeated. (This was the case in Example 13.) But what is a *meaningful* part of a hierarchy?

The complete label of a module (of depth d) within a hierarchy reads (see pages 54 f.):

$\underline{5}$ $s_0.s_1s_2...s_d;m_d$.

The total of the modules[2] springing from this module, i.e. the *rest hierarchy* determined by *the* module $\underline{5}$ is labeled:

(4)   Hierarchy $s_0.s_1s_2...s_d;m_d$,

with (4) containing the module $\underline{5}$.

Special cases of (4): if the rest hierarchy belongs to the hierarchy which contains the repetition regulation, s_0 can be omitted.

(5a)   Hierarchy $.s_1s_2...s_d;m_d$.

If the sequence $s_1s_2...s_d$ consists of only one module, m_d is unnecessary.

(5b)   Hierarchy $s_0.s_1s_2...s_d$.

If the rest hierarchy consists of only one sequence, we write instead of (5b):

(5c)   Sequence $s_0.s_1s_2...s_d$,

---

[1] See the expression **Hierarchy 5/6** in unit 007 on page 157, while taking into consideration expression $\underline{3}$ on this page.

[2] If the $s_0.s_1s_2...s_d$ - sequence is *structured*, m_d is the module number found by counting, starting with the first module of the *full sequence*.

or, if the requirement of (5a) is met:

(5d)   Sequence $s_1 s_2 ... s_d$.

If the rest hierarchies are modules, the following is valid accordingly

(5e)   Module $s_0 . s_1 s_2 ... s_t ; m_d$

or

(5f)   Module $s_1 s_2 ... s_d$.

If, finally, the rest hierarchy (4) is identical with the complete hierarchy, the following expression applies due to $d = 0$:

(5g)   Hierarchy s_0.

The labels of the following table refer to Example 11 (page 49 to 53):

Labels of Rest Hierarchies

Hierarchy Part	Modules Belonging to Hierarchy Part
26	26;1 26.1;1 26.2;1 26.2;2 26.2;3 26.21;1
26.1;1 = 26.1	26.1;1
26.2	26.2;1 26.2;2 26.2;3 26.21;1
26.2;1	26.2;1 26.21;1
26.2;2	26.2;2
26.2;3	26.2;3

Table 5

The labels given in the left column of the table describe meaningful parts of the instruction determined by the full hierarchy. These are *final parts*: instruction which begins with a certain module, and which is "deepened" according to the flow rules of the hierarchy and which can be returned to its point of departure.

The *general* repetition expression results from the "combination" of (5) with 5. It reads:

(6)   Hierarchy $s_0^1 . s_1^1 s_2^1 ... s_t^1 ; m_{d_1}^1 / s_0^2 . s_1^2 s_2^2 ... s_d^2 ; m_{d_2}^2 / ... / s_0^n . s_1^n s_2^n ... s_d^n ; m_{d_n}^n$.

(The expression "sequence 1/2" in Example 13 of the preceding Point (pages 64 to 66) results from (5d) and (6) together with $d = 1$. Due to 4 we can also write "sequence 1-2".)

Part Two

RESPONSE JUDGING

Chapter III

This chapter is an attempt to satisfy practical needs without neglecting the aspect of universality of concept formation. Questions of efficiency and/or of semantic-linguistic optimization of judging procedures will not be dealt with. We proceed from the assumption that any response judging is *fundamentally* a comparison of the learner's response (response string) with the judging strings preset by the instrugrammer, either explicitly or encoded, in a fixed or variable manner.

The two methods of response judging that were already applied in Part I, i.e. answer assessment with the partial and the equals key, will be discussed systematically. The partial key demands or forbids that the response contains certain judging strings. Since this requirement can be met by *parts* of the response, we will call this procedure *partial* judging. The *equals key* demands that the response equals either *one* or (if negated) *none* of the preset judging strings.

A judging structure is described in § 11 which includes partial judging (and therefore also equality judging) as a special case. I assume that this structure is universally valid and that all key types needed can be defined by the specification of its *type parameters*.

Set-theoretical specifications that appear throughout this chapter have only minor importance as regards the practice of instrugram construction. This also applies to the generalizations of § 10 Point 5 and, in particular, § 11. These can be skipped over on first reading.

§ 8 Single-String Keys

Single-string keys contain exactly one *judging string* J.

1. Single-String Partial Key[1]
The key

(1) A,h_A: J

requires that the learner's response *contains* the judging string J.
   In other words, the learner's response L has the form

$$L = \ \ \dots J \dots \ .$$

If, for example, J = 'red', then (1) is fulfilled by all responses of the form

$$L = \ \ \dots \text{red} \dots \ .$$

There can but does not have to be something in front of or after 'red', e.g.
'bright red', 'red flower' etc., or simply 'red'.
   The *precise* formulation of the key-requirement (1) is somewhat more
complicated. The learner's responses L which belong to the set

(2) $\{ XJY \mid X \in B, Y \in B \}$

have the answer attribute A determined by (1).[2] B indicates the basic set of
responses that can be submitted in the given input system, i.e. that can be fed
in using the given input medium; digits and spaces will be excluded for the
time being (see pages 82 ff., Points 1 and 2). The expression XJY represents
the *concatenation* of X, J and Y.[3] (If X = 'bow', J = '-' and Y = 'wow', then
XJY = 'bow-wow'.) The string variables X and Y are *independent* of each
other and according to (2) can have any value out of B. The same holds true
for all partial keys.
   Note that B also includes the "empty response" or *zero-string* θ: the *first*
response of the module is an empty response, if just the FINISHED-sign is
input (on the computer by pressing RETURN); any non-first response is an
empty one if the learner *deletes* the previous response. If X = θ and Y = θ,
then

$$XJY = \theta J \theta = J.$$

Consequently, the learner's response L = J also meets requirement (1).

---

[1] See Example 1 on page 23.

[2] The sign $\in$ stands for *is an element of.*

[3] If Q has the form XJY, then J is contained in Q. Thus, J = 'ank' is contained in
Q = 'Frankfurt' because Q = X'ank'Y; 'kurt' on the contrary is *not* contained in 'Frankfurt'.
Besides, if a string J is contained in a string Q, J is called *partial string* of Q.

The *negated* single-string partial key has the form

(3) $A,h_A:$ **Not J.**

The key forbids the occurrence of the judging string J in the response. It is fulfilled by all those responses that do not comply with key (1). Key (3) is the negative of key (1). (3) in detail reads:

$$\text{Not } (A,h_A: \text{ J}).$$

In terms of set theory, the answer attribute A required by (3) is determined by

(4) $B - \{XJY \mid X \in B, Y \in B\},$

i.e. by the *complement* of (2). All responses which belong to the basic set B but not to set (2) have the attribute (3).

2. Single-String Equals Key[1]

The single-string *equals key*

(5) $A,h_A = \text{ J}$

commands that the learner's answer L *equals* the judging string J:

$$L = J.$$

This follows from (2) if X and Y are zero-strings (see above). (The set of responses belonging to (5) contains exactly one element.)

The meaning of the negated equals key (of the non-equality key)

(6a) $A,h_A = \text{ Not J},$

or, in a different form,

(6b) $A,h_A \neq \text{ J}$

is obvious: the learner's answer has to be different from J:

$$L \neq J.$$

Or, written now as a special case of (4), the elements of

$$B - \{J\}$$

and only they are the desired responses.[2]

---

[1] See Example 2 on page 25 f.

[2] The set $\{J\}$ contains the string J and nothing else.

§ 9 Multiple-String Keys

1. Before-Key
If the response is to contain the judging string 'red' *before* the judging string 'green', i.e. if the response is to have the form

$$... \text{red} ... \text{green} ...,$$

this requirement could most easily be expressed as[1]

$$: \quad (\text{'red'}, \text{'green'}).$$

More generally, a response in the form of

$$\underline{1} \qquad\qquad ... J_1 ... J_2 ...$$

could be required by

$$\underline{2} \qquad\qquad : \quad (J_1, J_2).$$

However, for reasons of better readability, let us agree on the following mode of expression:

$$\underline{3} \qquad\qquad : \quad \textbf{Before}(J_1, J_2).$$

The meaning of $\underline{3}$ (and $\underline{2}$ accordingly) follows from $\underline{1}$.
a) J_1 does not have to occur immediately before J_2.
b) J_1 and J_2 must *not overlap* each other.
c) The key only demands that J_1 occurs before J_2; however, J_2 *may* also precede J_1. Hence responses in the form of $... J_2 ... J_1 ... J_2 ...$ are also acceptable.
d) The **Before**-condition can *only* be fulfilled if both J_1 and J_2 are contained in the response.

The general (non-negated) n-string **Before**-key reads:

$$(7) \qquad\qquad A, h_A: \quad \textbf{Before}(J_1,...,J_n).$$

The learner responses L required by (7) have the form

$$L = ... J_1 ... J_2 ... J_3 ... \;\; ... \;\; ... J_n ...$$

or, to be more precise

$$(8) \qquad L \in \{X_0 J_1 X_1 J_2 X_2 J_3 X_3 ... X_{t-1} J_t X_t ... X_{n-1} J_n X_n \mid X_t \in B\}.$$

As can easily be seen from (8), the (non-negated) single-string partial key (1) is contained in (7) as the special case $n=1$. We therefore agree on

$$(9) \qquad\qquad \textbf{Before } J = J.$$

---

[1] Sometimes we leave out of the key representation the key *name* and the corresponding *specific high number*.

In the case of $X_t = \theta$ (for all t) we obtain in (8) a one-element set

$$\{J_1 J_2 J_3 \dots J_n\}$$

with the element

$$J = J_1 J_2 J_3 \dots J_n.$$

The key

<u>4</u> $E, h_E = $ **Before**$(J_1, \dots, J_n)$

will therefore be given the meaning of the equals key (5) on page 73:

$$A, h_A = J$$

with

$$J = J_1 J_2 \dots J_n.$$

That is, after the equals sign, **Before** takes on the meaning of a concatenation operator.

The negated **Before**-key

(10) $A, h_A:$ **Not Before**$(J_1, \dots, J_n)$

indicates the complement of set (8). In the case of n=2, (10) requires that J_1 does not occur before J_2 in the learner's response; if the response contains J_2, it has the form

$$L = X J_2 X',$$

with X *not* including string J_1.[1]

The negation of <u>4</u> reads:

$$E, h_E = \text{ Not Before}(J_1, \dots, J_n)$$

and requires that the response is different from the string J consisting of the strings $J_1, J_2, \dots, J_n$:

$$L \neq J.$$

2. And-Partial Key

The requirement that the answer should contain the strings J *and* J' is expressed by:

<u>5a</u> $A, h_A:$ **And**(J, J')

or

<u>5b</u> $A, h_A:$ J & J'.

The following learner responses fulfil requirement <u>5</u>:

---

[1] X and X' are also − like X_t − string variables.

<u>6</u>   L ϵ {XJY | X ϵ B & Y ϵ B} $\cap$ {X'J'Y'| X' ϵ B & Y' ϵ B}.

By comparing this expression with (2), we realize that it equals the set of all responses containing J *intersected* with the set of all responses containing J': all responses which contain both J and J' are included in <u>6</u>.

We generalize the **And**-key <u>5</u> by replacing the two judging strings with as many **Before**-expressions as desired, each containing an arbitrary number of judging strings. We get the following structure:[1]

(11) A,h$_A$: **And[Before(...), ..., Before(...)]**.

Expression (11) includes both the **Before**-partial key (7) and the **And**-key

(12) A,h$_A$: **And(J, J', J", ...)**,

which contains as many judging strings as desired (but no **Before**-connection). Expression (11) is *defined* as the **And**-connection of arbitrarily many keys according to (7).

It should be added that

                    And J = J.

3. Or-Partial Key

Let us begin again with the very simple example of two judging strings J and J'.

<u>7a</u> A,h$_A$: **Or(J, J')**

or

<u>7b</u> A,h$_A$: **J v J'**.

Expression <u>7</u> requires that J or J' occur in the response. The **Or** — as is common practice in logic — is to be understood as *inclusive*; expression <u>7</u> does not demand that the response should contain *either* J or J'. The answer attribute A required by <u>7</u> is determined by the following <u>union of sets</u>:

<u>8</u>   {XJY | X ϵ B & Y ϵ B} $\cup$ {X'J'Y'| X' ϵ B & Y' ϵ B}.

Set <u>8</u> includes all responses which contain J or J' (or both). In other words, set union <u>8</u> includes all responses in which at least one of the strings J or J' occurs.

By analogy with Point 2, we form the generalization of <u>7</u> so as to contain arbitrarily many **Before**-expressions with arbitrarily many judging strings:

---

[1] Any reader interested in a general key representation is referred to § 11 (page 88).

(13) $\qquad A,h_A:$ **Or[Before(...), ..., Before(...)]**,

which is defined as the **Or**-connection of **Before**-keys (7). Special cases of (13) are firstly key (7) and secondly

(14) $\qquad\qquad\qquad A,h_A:$ **Or(J, J', J", ...).**

By analogy with Points 1 and 2, the following holds:

(15) $\qquad\qquad\qquad$ **Or J = And J = Before J = J.**

4. The Negations of the And- and the Or-Partial Key

According to the laws of DE MORGAN[1], the negations of the **And**-partial key (11) and the **Or**-partial key (13) result in:

(16) $\qquad\qquad A,h_A:$ **Or[Not Before(...), ..., Not Before(...)]**

resp.

(17) $\qquad\qquad A,h_A:$ **And[Not Before(...), ..., Not Before(...)].**

Thus, the negated **And**- and **Or**-partial keys are found corresponding to the negation of the **Before**-key (see (10)).

5. General Partial Key [2]

With each of the two following keys (we will only note down the key kernels):

(18) **Or{And[±Before(..),..,±Before(..)], . ., And[±Before(..),..,±Before(..)]}**
or
(19) **And{Or[±Before(..),..,±Before(..)], . ., Or[±Before(..),..,±Before(..)]}**

any partial response conditions can be represented. Before we justify proposition (18) we should explain the meaning of "± **Before**(..)". Firstly, it means that *either* a plus *or* a minus sign is placed in front of **Before**. Secondly,

$$\textbf{+ Before(..) = Before(..)}$$

and

$$\textbf{-Before(..) = Not Before(..).}$$

---

[1] DE MORGAN's laws: the negation of the And-connection of propositions equals the Or-connection of the propositions' negations. The negation of the Or-connection of propositions equals the And-connection of the propositions' negations.

[2] a) This section can be skipped over on first reading. b) The braces used in (18) and (19) have normal meaning; they do not indicate sets. c) Being short of place we note in (18) and (19) just two dots (instead of the customary three).

Let us now look at the reasons for the universality of (18).[1] To transform *any* given key kernel so as to have the form (18), we must proceed as follows:

a) Firstly, we eliminate the negations of conjunctions (**And**-connections) and adjunctions (**Or**-connections) with the help of DE MORGAN's laws. Thus, the only negations remaining are those of **Before**-connections.

b) Since (18) is an adjunction of conjunctions of **Before**-connections and/or negations of **Before**-connections, we only have to transform the remaining conjunctions of adjunctions into adjunctions of conjunctions. This can be done with the help of the conjunctive distributive law of propositional logic[2]

$$(20) \qquad\qquad (A \vee B) \& C = (A \& C) \vee (B \& C).$$

By systematically applying this law, all **And**-connections of **Or**-connections can be transformed into **Or**-connections of **And**-connections. Finally, we arrive at structure (18).

6. Equals Key

a) The *general equals key* has the following form:

$$(21) \qquad\qquad A,h_A = \pm Or(J_1, ..., J_n),$$

that is: every equals key can be represented either by

$$(21a) \qquad\qquad\qquad = Or(J_1, ..., J_n)$$

or by

$$(21b) \qquad\qquad\qquad = Not\ Or(J_1, ..., J_n).$$

The meaning of (21a) and (21b) is quite simple. The responses that correspond to (21a) read:

$$L = J_1 \ or \ L = J_2 \ or \ L = J_3 \ etc.$$

The learner's response must be identical with precisely one of the judging strings contained in the key kernel. Key (21b) requires

$$L \neq J_1 \ and \ L \neq J_2 \ and \ L \neq J_3 \ etc.$$

The response must not be identical with any of the preset strings.

---

[1] The reasons for the universality of (19) are analogous.

[2] Sometimes also called *statement logic* or *sentential logic*.

b) *Special Equals Keys*

The requirement that a response should be made up of the strings J_1 and J_2 (without overlapping), i.e. that it should equal J_1J_2 or J_2J_1, explicitly reads

$$\underline{9} \qquad\qquad A,h_A = \ \text{Or}(J_1J_2, J_2J_1),$$

and is therefore a special case of (21a). We abbreviate $\underline{9}$ to

$$\underline{10} \qquad\qquad A,h_A = \ \underline{\text{And}}(J_1, J_2).$$

The underlining indicates that it is *not* the **And** of propositional logic which is meant here.[1] Key $\underline{10}$ requires that the response contains the strings J_1 and J_2 exactly once, and *nothing else*. This means that the response equals either J_1J_2 or J_2J_1. The general **And**-equals key

$$(22a) \qquad\qquad A,h_A = \ \underline{\text{And}}(n_1J_1, n_2J_2, ..., n_mJ_m)$$

requires that the answer should be made up of precisely n_1 J_1-strings, n_2 J_2-strings, n_3 J_3-strings, ... *and* n_m J_m-strings. If this is to be ruled out, we say:

$$(22b) \qquad\qquad A,h_A = \ \text{Not } \underline{\text{And}}(n_1J_1, n_2J_2, ..., n_mJ_m) \ .$$

The requirement

$$\underline{11} \qquad\qquad = \ \text{Or}(J_1, J_2, J_1J_2, J_2J_1)$$

demands less than $\underline{9}$. It is also met by the learner responses

$$L = J_1 \ \text{ and } \ L = J_2.$$

We abbreviate $\underline{11}$ to

$$\underline{12} \qquad\qquad = \ \underline{\text{Or}}(J_1, J_2).$$

In words, $\underline{12}$ can be described as follows: the response must consist of precisely one J_1-string *and/or* of precisely one J_2-string. (Again, the underlined **Or** is not the **Or** of propositional logic!) The generalization of $\underline{12}$

$$(23a) \qquad\qquad A,h_A = \ \underline{\text{Or}}(n_1J_1, n_2J_2, ..., n_mJ_m)$$

requires that the response should be made up of at least *one* but no more than n_1 J_1-strings and/or of at least *one* but no more than n_2 J_2-strings, ... and/or of at least *one* but no more than n_m J_m-strings.

Requirement (23a) is met, for example, by J_1 only, J_2 only etc., and (at the other end of the spectrum) also by responses that fulfil (22a).

---

[1] Key $\underline{10}$ cannot be explained as a conjunction of single-string keys: if $L = J_1$, then $L = J_2$ is not possible at the same time (except for the trivial case of $J_1 = J_2$).

The meaning of the key

(23b) $A,\mathrm{h}_A = \ \mathrm{Not}\ \underline{\mathrm{Or}}(\mathrm{n}_1\mathrm{J}_1, \mathrm{n}_2\mathrm{J}_2, ..., \mathrm{n}_m\mathrm{J}_m)$

follows on from what has been said above.

7. Frequency

The requirement that e.g. the judging string 'red' is to occur in the response means that 'red' is to occur at least once. If 'red' is to occur *at least* twice, we write

: **Before**('red', 'red').

We abbreviate this to

: 2 'red'.

Accordingly, we abbreviate

: **Before**('2', '2', '2', '2')

to

: 4 '2',

which means: the digit '2' is to occur at least four times in the response. (Please note the difference between the *number* 4 and the *numeral* '2'.)

The general key for the minimum frequency n of a string J

(24) A,h_A: n J   (n: natural number)

is a special case of (7) with $\mathrm{J} = \mathrm{J}_1 = ... = \mathrm{J}_n$. It requires that the string J is to occur at least n times in the response.

The key for the *maximum frequency* n of the string J reads

(25) A,h_A: **Not**[(n + 1)J].

The negation of the minimum frequency (n + 1) yields the maximum frequency n. Proceeding from (24) and (25), the *exact* frequency n of string J can be demanded by

A,h_A: **And**{nJ, **Not**[(n + 1)J]}.

We abbreviate this to

(26) A,h_A: **Exact** nJ.

Key (26) requires that the string J occurs *exactly* n times in the response.[1]

---

[1] Please note that the **Exact**-key relating to J does not say anything about strings *different* from J: the **Exact**-key is not an equals key.

Important generalizations of (24) and (26) are

(27) A,h_A: $\textbf{Before}(n_1 J_1, ..., n_m J_m)$

and

(28) A,h_A: $\textbf{Before}(\textbf{Exact } n_1 J_1, ..., \textbf{Exact } n_m J_m)$.

Thus, the required responses must have the following structure:

$$\ldots J_1 \ldots J_1 \ldots J_2 \ldots J_2 \ldots \qquad \ldots J_m \ldots J_m \ldots$$
$$\underset{J_1\text{-strings}}{n_1} \quad \underset{J_2\text{-strings}}{n_2} \qquad\qquad \underset{J_m\text{-strings}}{n_m}$$

Key (27) permits further J_1-, J_2-, J_3-strings etc. at different locations, key (28) does not permit that.

8. Order

To ensure that the strings J_1, J_2, J_3, ..., J_n (provided they, or some of them, occur in a response) occur in this order, we have to require for, e.g., the case $n=3$ that neither J_2 occurs before J_1 nor J_3 before J_1 nor J_3 before J_2. In general, a judging string with a higher index must not occur before a judging string with a smaller index. The response must not contain any partial string of the form

$$J_t \ldots J_{t'}$$

if $t > t'$. We abbreviate the corresponding judging requirement to

(29) A,h_A: $\textbf{Order}(J_1, ..., J_n)$.

If the occurrence of J_1 to J_n is to be *guaranteed*, the key kernel must be complemented conjunctively by $\textbf{Before}(J_1, ..., J_n)$:

(30) A,h_A: $\textbf{And}[\textbf{Order}(J_1, ..., J_n), \textbf{Before}(J_1, ..., J_n)]$.

If each of the strings J_1, J_2, J_3 etc. to J_n is to occur *exactly once* in this order, then the judging requirement reads

(31) A,h_A: $\textbf{And}[\textbf{Order}(J_1, ..., J_n), \textbf{Exact}(J_1, ..., J_n)]$.

9. Determination of the Model Answer and the Model Comment
   via the R1-Kernel (Postscript to Chapter I)

The R1-kernel is to determine the model answer whenever the auxiliary section is empty or the expression 'model answer' does not occur in the auxiliary section (see page 38).

In this case the R1-key must have one of the following forms:

<u>13a</u>	**R1,1: J,**
<u>13b</u>	**R1,1: J v K,**
<u>13c</u>	**R1,1 = J,**
<u>14</u>	**R1,1 = <u>And</u> $(J_1, ..., J_n)$.**

K is any key kernel. The strings J, J_1, ..., J_n must be plain-text strings. For the cases <u>13</u> the model answer equals the plain-text string J. In the case of the strict key <u>14</u> the model comment for $A \dagger R$ differs from the one given in Table 2 on page 37. It reads:

> *A*-**St-final comment.** Any answer consisting of $J_1, J_2, ..., J_{n-1}$ and J_n is correct (e.g. the answer: $J_1 J_2 ... J_n$).
> **Addition.**

§ 10 Tolerances and Intolerances

We have, until now, excluded spaces and digits from our considerations (see page 72, penultimate paragraph). The reason is that judging spaces is fundamentally handled *more tolerantly*, and the judging of digits *more strictly* than that of other signs. *Fundamentally* means that we consider this as *normal* and therefore do not indicate it in the instrugram.

We call such agreements *universal* and distinguish them from *optional* regulations. In contrast to the former, the latter must be indicated in the instrugram to become valid. Depending on their range, we distinguish between three kinds of optional regulations:

— *Global* regulations are valid for the whole instrugram; they are noted down in the *lead-in to the instrugram*;

— *Local* regulations are valid for one unit (module, sequence or hierarchy); they will only take effect if the corresponding head says so;

— *On-the-spot* regulations are valid for one dialogue element and are determined in the key.

On-the-spot regulations can override local and global regulations at a given point, local regulations can override global regulations *locally*.

1. Spaces

The main task of the space is word limitation:[1] a word is a string of signs which is limited by spaces (and does not contain any internal spaces). However, it has to be taken into account that limitation of words can also be

---

[1] The role of spaces in layout is not considered here (e.g. spaces used for centering and paragraph or section formation etc.).

achieved by other signs such as the full stop, semicolon, comma, colon, exclamation and question mark. Moreover we have to consider what effect a *missing* hyphen has at the end of a line: (a) end of line becomes end of word and (b) beginning of next line becomes beginning of next word.

Therefore we adopt the following universal *convention on spaces*:

(32)   The beginning or finishing space required together with a judging string may be replaced with another *word limitator* in the response; it may be left out completely if the judging string is either the beginning or the end of the response.

Normal[1] word limitators are

full stop, semicolon, comma, colon, exclamation and question mark.

The instrugram author can deviate from this norm both *globally* and *locally* by noting down *his* word limitators in the *lead-in* to the instrugram or the head of the unit respectively. If, for example, the author wants to exclude the exclamation mark (because of its mathematical meaning) and to include the slash, this can be done by

(32a) **word limitator**: full stop, semicolon, comma, colon, slash, question mark.

As an addition to the universal basic tolerance (32), we define two *optional* tolerances of spaces which can take effect both globally and locally.

Half-Tolerance of Spaces

(33)   The string of spaces required together with a judging string may be extended as desired, or shortened to one position (each) or omitted completely in the response, unless both neighbors are either a) letters or b) digits.[2]

The half-tolerance does not affect words made up of either letters or digits. This is not true for the following:

Full Tolerance of Spaces

(34)   Spaces occurring in the response are ignored. This does not apply to *exempted* terms.

---

[1] *Normal* in the sense it is used in the introductory remarks to § 10 on page 82.

[2] This means that the requirement '5 km' would also be met by the response '5km'.

Half-tolerances and full tolerances are significant in judging mathematical and other formula-like responses. Spaces usually play only a minor role here, in contrast to verbal responses. If strings such as the names of transcendental functions (e.g. 'sin' or 'cos') are to be *exempted* from full tolerance, then this will be noted down in the lead-in to the instrugram.

2. Digits
To combine the (desired) freedom of verbal formulation with the precision requirement of preset numerical values, we adopt the universal

Digit-Judging Convention:

(35) Digit strings which are part of a judging string required by a partial key do not only have to appear in the response; furthermore it is essential that the total number of all response digits equals the total number of all judging digits.

If, for example, the length of a ten-meter distance is asked for, the response '110 m' containing the digit-string '10' is to be forbidden but any text (i.e. strings consisting of letters and special signs) *before* and/or *after* '10 m' is to be permitted. This is achieved by the requirement

$$: \text{ '10 m'}$$

in connection with (35). In contrast, the requirement

$$= \text{ '10 m'}$$

would forbid free-formulated additions. Convention (35) has the effect — except for cases completely insignificant in practice — that digit strings occurring in the partial key are judged in a *strict* manner.

3. Plain-Text Convention
In partial keys, judging strings can occur in a very fragmentary form. The judging string 'interr', for instance, can cover several responses such as 'interrupt', 'interrupted', 'interrupts', 'interrupting' etc. For the benefit of the instrugram reader, we agree that such fragments must be supplemented by the author's plain text. If this is the word ' interrupt ', the required key kernel reads:

<u>1</u>   ' interrupt ' v ' interr'

Since 'interr' is contained in ' interrupt ', the key kernels <u>1</u> and

' interr'

are equivalent as *partial* key kernels. The plain-text addition by means of adjunction (i.e. via *or*) does not affect the judging process. We adopt the following:

(36)   Fragmentary judging strings (which do not contain digits) are to be supplemented *adjunctively* by plain text. The plain-text string must a) contain the fragment as partial string and b) occur in the key kernel before the corresponding fragment.

4. Small or Capital Letters

We regulate the equal treatment of small and capital letters *globally* and/or *locally* by

(37a)   **Tolerance**: small/capital letters.

The normal case, i.e. the unequal treatment of small and capital letters, is achieved *globally* if *nothing* is said in the lead-in to the instrugram concerning the use of small or capital letters. This global intolerance can be *locally* invalidated with the help of (37a). Global tolerance is locally suspended by

(37b)   **Intolerance**: small/capital letters

If the global or local tolerance is to be invalidated *on the spot*, i.e. for a single dialogue element, this can be done by underlining the *names* of the judging strings in question, e.g.,

(38)   'Germany'.

The reverse, i.e. on-the-spot tolerance of the use of small or capital letters — with global or local intolerance —, is indicated by a broken line. Thus, for example,

(39)   'Commonwealth of Independent States'

(among others) permits the responses:

COMMONWEALTH OF INDEPENDENT STATES,
commonwealth of independent states,
Commonwealth of independent states,
Commonwealth of independent States,
Commonwealth of Independent States.

The judging string (39) can be written down in many different ways without any effect on the response judging. (Each small letter could be replaced with the corresponding capital and vice versa.) However, the given written form is relevant for the *model answer*. (The latter is identical with the R1-kernel if it has not been noted down in the auxiliary section; this has been specified on page 81 f. in Point 9.) Please note that the underlining is *not* part of the judging string. If the learner is permitted to use small and capital letters at will and the model answer reads "Commonwealth of Independent States", then (39) must be required.

5. Numerical Value[1]
In this section only on-the-spot regulations will be discussed.

a) *Precise Value*
The key

(40) $$A,h_A = \sqrt{3}$$

requires any response which expresses the numerical value $\sqrt{3}$ with the highest possible precision. (The latter is determined by input and judging system.)

b) *Rounding Tolerance*
The key

(41) $$A,h_A = \textbf{Around } 2$$

requires a string S whose value lies between 1.5 and 2.5 or, to be more precise, for whom the following is correct:

$$1.5 \le \text{Value S} < 2.5.$$

The general value tolerance is expressed in one of the following ways:

(42) $$A,h_A = \begin{bmatrix} a < & < b \\ a < & \le b \\ a \le & < b \\ a \le & \le b \end{bmatrix}$$

Hereby a and b are any numbers for which $a < b$ is correct. The key kernel

$$a < \quad < b$$

means that

$$a < \text{Value S} < b.$$

By analogy, this also goes for the other kernels of (42).
   In comparison to (42), the keys (43) require in addition that the response is a *string of digits* (with or without a decimal point).

(43) $$A,h_A = \begin{bmatrix} a < \textbf{ string of digits } < b \\ a < \textbf{ string of digits } \le b \\ a \le \textbf{ string of digits } < b \\ a \le \textbf{ string of digits } \le b \end{bmatrix}$$

---

[1] We are only talking about the equals key here. However, there is a corresponding partial key to each of these keys: while the equals keys only permit numerical responses with certain numerical values, the corresponding partial keys permit additional text strings without numerical values (see, for example, subsequence [1] on page 169 in Appendix B).

c) *Number of Decimal Places*
With

(44)
> **Decimal places > n,**
> **Decimal places = n,**
> **Decimal places < n**

we require a response which is a *decimal string* with more than, equal to, or less than n places behind the decimal point (which could also be a comma). Thus, the key

$$\underline{2} \qquad A,h_A = \text{ Around 3.2 \& Decimal places < 3}$$

requires one of the following responses

3.15; 3.16; 3.17; 3.18; 3.19; 3.2; 3.20; 3.21; 3.22; 3.23; 3.24.

The response '3.235', which fulfills the requirement **Around** 3.2 is forbidden by $\underline{2}$. The last of the requirements (44) is of special importance in practice. It can be used to counteract the widespread bad habit of producing pseudo-accuracies.

6. Commutativity of Mathematical Terms

If a) the factors of a product, b) the addends of a sum, and c) the members of an equation may be interchanged, we express this *on the spot* by

(45) **Commutation J.**

J stands for the product, the sum or the equation respectively. If, for example,

$$J = \text{ '2x - y = 0'}$$

it follows that

Commutation J = Or('2x - y = 0', 'x · 2 - y = 0', '-y + 2x = 0',

'-y + x · 2 = 0', '0 = 2x - y', '0 = -y + 2x',

'0 = x · 2 - y', '0 = -y +x · 2').

If the commutativity is to be valid globally or locally, we note down

(46) **Commutativity.**

If the commutativity is to be valid for addends *only* or for factors *only* or for the members of an equation *only*, we write in the key

(47)
> **Addend commutation,**
> **Factor commutation,**
> **Side commutation,**

or in the head or in the lead-in to the instrugram respectively:

(48)
Addend commutativity,
Factor commutativity,
Side commutativity.

If tolerances are to be invalidated on the spot, this is achieved by "underdotting". In the key one of the following notions is noted:

Commutation,

Addend commutation,

Factor commutation,

Side commutation.

This procedure can be made universally applicable to tolerances *still to be defined* in an analogous way. (It could also have been applied to the question of small or capital letters but at the expense of an increased writing workload.)

§ 11 Universal Response Key: Type Parameters, Judging Strings and Judging-String Variables

I believe that any response is contained in the set[1]

$$(49) \quad \sum_{u=1}^{U} \pi_{i=1.}^{I} [+/-]^{iu} \{ X_0^{iu} J_1^{iu} X_1^{iu} \dots X_{t-1}^{iu} J_t^{iu} X_t^{iu} \dots X_{n_{iu}-1}^{iu} J_{n_{iu}}^{iu} X_{n_{iu}}^{iu} | X_t^{iu} \in S_t^{iu} \}.$$

Set (49) represents the general answer attribute. The *judging type* is determined by the *type parameters* X_t^{iu}. The type parameters determine the *procedure*[2] *how* the response is to be compared with the judging strings J_t^{iu}: the X_t^{iu} determine *how*, the J_t^{iu} *what with*.

The key type of equality judging can be derived from (49) with $S_t^{iu} = \{\theta\}$ for all t, i and u, i.e. with

$$(50) \qquad\qquad X_t^{iu} = \theta.$$

This causes solely one-element sets in (49):

$$\{ J_1^{iu} \dots J_t^{iu} \dots J_n^{iu} \} = \{ J^{iu} \}.$$

---

[1] Set (49) is a generalization of expression (8) on page 74. The plus-minus sign combination $[+/-]^{iu}$ has the following meaning: a) Before the *set brace either* the plus *or* the minus sign is placed (for a certain (i,u)). b) The minus sign has the effect of the complement formation of the set in the braces; the plus sign does not have any effect, it can be omitted. The sum sign Σ stands for union of the sets, and the product sign π for their intersection. U and I_u are the numbers of sets to be united or intersected, respectively.

[2] Judging logic specified in the form of flowcharts.

That is, (49) either takes the form[1]

(51a) $\Sigma \{J^u\}$

or the form

(51b) $\pi \overline{\{J^i\}} = \overline{\Sigma \{J^i\}}.$

(The overlining indicates the complement formation.) Expressions (51a) and (51b) are the set-theoretical analogues to (21a) and (21b) respectively on page 78: the union corresponds to the **Or** of propositional logic, the complement of the union to the *negation* of the **Or**.

If none of the judging strings contains digits, the *partial key* can be derived from (49), with the judging parameters assuming any values from the basic set B, i.e. with

<u>1</u> $S_t^{iu} = B$

for all t, i and u. If digits occur in at least one of the judging strings, then X_t^{iu} must not contain any digits due to the digit-judging convention (page 84):

<u>2</u> $S_t^{iu} = B - D,$

D is the set of the digit strings. It should also be noted that the type parameters of the partial key are *independent* of one another.

(52)   We can derive the universal partial key from (49) if we let the X_t^{iu} assume independently any values from sets <u>1</u> and <u>2</u>.

In order to realize the equivalence of structure (18) with the set of responses determined by (52), the reader should bear in mind that
a) the union corresponds to the **Or**,
b) the intersection corresponds to the **And,** and
c) the complement formation corresponds to the negation.
In addition, expression (8) should be viewed as the definition of the **Before-key** (7).

Further key types are the "beginning" and the "end key", being special cases of the partial key. They require that the response either begins or ends with a certain string. These two types are determined by

<u>3</u> $X_0^{iu} = \theta$ or $X_{n_{iu}}^{iu} = \theta$

respectively.

Of course, key types can be combined, e.g. by the requirement that *both* conditions <u>3</u> must be met, or by a "mixture" of partial and equals key: a

---

[1] The trivial cases of a) the empty set, and b) the basic set B have not been taken into consideration.

response might be required which either is identical to a certain judging string *or* contains other judging strings. The type parameters are then partly identical with the empty string and partly arbitrary.

Until now, we regarded the judging strings J_t^{iu} as *constants*. However, this can be different. Judging-string *variables* occur when the learner is free to choose from a pregiven set. If, for example, J is a judging-string variable whose range is determined by the small letters

<u>4</u> $S = \{\text{'a','b','c',...,'z'}\}$,

the following equals key

<u>5</u> $A, h_A = J + J = 2J$

requires as a response an element from the set

$$\{J + J = 2J \mid J \in S\},$$

i.e. 'a + a = 2a' *or* 'b + b = 2b' *or* 'c + c = 2c' etc. In principle, key <u>5</u> could therefore also be written as the Or-combination of constant judging strings. Such a representation is not recommendable due to practical reasons. (We need *variables* to ensure readability. This is made particularly clear in the case of *infinite* ranges.)

The ranges of the judging-string variables are given in the auxiliary section. (For example, definition <u>4</u> is recorded there.) Variables whose ranges are not specified can assume any value from the basic set.

To emphasize the difference between judging strings (or judging-string variables) and type parameters, key <u>5</u> is brought into the form of (49), which in our case is identical with (8) on page 74:

<u>6</u> $X_0\, J_1\, X_1\, J_2\, X_2\, J_3\, X_3\, J_4\, X_4\, J_5\, X_5\, J_6\, X_6$;

<u>7</u> $\theta\ J\ \theta\ +\ \theta\ J\ \theta\ =\ \theta\ 2\ \theta\ J\ \theta$.

The comparison of the variables <u>6</u> with their values <u>7</u> underneath yields:

$X_t = \theta$ for t=0,1,2,3,4,5,6	Key-type parameter
$J_1 = J_3 = J_6 = J$	Variable judging string
$J_2 = \text{'+'}$	Constant judging string
$J_4 = \text{' = '}$	Constant judging string
$J_5 = \text{'2'}$	Constant judging string

If we agree — according to (34) — on a *tolerance of spaces* for <u>5</u>, the X_t-parameters in <u>6</u> will consequently be *zero-strings or strings of spaces*.

Part Three

FULL DIDACTIC
REPRESENTATION OF INSTRUCTION

Improving
Readability and Testability

The significance of the elementary description developed in Part One of this book lies in its universality: it is designed so as to make any instruction representable. Since Instruction Language has, in particular, to meet the needs of practical application, and instrugrams designed with the concepts of the language have to fulfil the basic demands of good readability, testability and improvability, abbreviations are needed for (elementary and therefore longish) representations of typical recurrent features. We call them *instructional types* and record them (see Figure 7 on page 34) in the head of the instructional unit.

The dialogue of a module can be rendered in strictly elementary or strictly typological representation, or in a *mixture* of both. By speaking of full didactic representation, we emphasize that those expressional devices of Instruction Language which are available are made full use of, and that the general has to be represented in general terms (typologically) and the individual in individual terms (elementarily) in order to achieve a readable and user-friendly representation of instruction.

A mixed representation is called *hybrid* if the individual and elementary *competes* with the typological and general: the schematizing effect of the instructional type is limited by the individual and thus partially invalidated.

The difference should be noted between the notion of the instructional type and that of the content-related, methodical sequence heading (discussed in Chapter II on page 45). Both serve the purpose of structuring contents and thus ensure good readability. However, the instructional type has above all the function of determining instruction, whereas the sequence heading relates to contents and/or method and does not affect the flow logic.

Part Three introduces several *examples* of abbreviations and abbreviation *methods*. A systematic approach has not been developed, let alone a complete system. As we noted in the Introduction, the language shell is *flexible* and *open*. Only suggestions are made. Practical application will show whether and how they have to be improved.

Chapter IV

INSTRUCTIONAL TYPES

The concept of the instructional type is introduced and explained by means of a simple example in § 12. Several response selection types are defined. The structure of the instructional unit's head and especially of the sequence head will be discussed in detail. In § 13 the instructional types of free, unequivocal, injective and bijective matching are described, following basic set theory. The main task of the selection types in both a narrow (§ 12) and a broader sense (§ 13) is to make an explicit representation of the *inadmissible*-dialogue unnecessary.

Furthermore, instructional types that determine the *entire* dialogue are introduced in § 14. The body of such modules only contains the theme. An instructional dialogue defined exclusively by the instructional type is called a *standard dialogue*. We will distinguish three variants. The simplest one is the rough standard, indicating only *whether* the response is correct, incorrect, or inadmissible. The frequency standard provides further information as to *how many* correct and how many incorrect signs are contained in the response. The fine standard assesses every single response element as correct or incorrect.

To define a standard dialogue we need the notion *dialogue variable*. But this device has a broader function. We also need it for less radical (and more interesting) simplifications of dialogue parts. It is used, for example, in coining *free-response* types. Further tools of optimizing representation introduced in § 14 are the set key, the text and set indicators, which make full use of the structure of the instrugram and the encoding of the model answer.

§ 12 Selection Types and Head Structure

Questions whose responses are limited to certain preset signs, i.e. *response indicators*, are called selection questions, their corresponding responses *selection responses*. Modules only permitting selection responses are called selection-response modules. In this paragraph we will discuss the *instructional types* **single selection, double selection, triple selection** etc. (The learner has to select exactly one, two, three etc. response indicators.) Furthermore, we will discuss the **free selection** and the **common selection** (in several variants).

1. Single Selection
With the help of the instructional type **single selection** the representation of Example 7 (page 38 f.) can be further simplified.[1]

Single Selection

003.   *Expansion Through Warming Up.*
       Single Selection; A..D.

       The metal lid of a jam jar is difficult to unscrew. How can we open the jar without breaking it?
       Choose one of the following answers, using its identification letter.[2]

       A. Force the lid off the jar with a screwdriver.
       B. Run hot water over the jar but not over the lid.
       C. Run hot water over the lid.
       D. Run cold water over the lid.

       Addition: Hot water warms up the lid. Since it consists of metal, it will expand and can therefore be screwed off more easily.

---

[1] We will now consider the example as a *sequence* in order to note down the sequence heading. (That is why '03' is now replaced by the three-digit label '003'.)

[2] Instead of identification letters we speak, as said above, more generally of response indicators.

R1,1 = 'C'
W1,2 = 'A'
This method is too forceful. The jar might break.
W2,2 = 'B'
St. If hot water runs over the jar it will expand slightly, and the lid will not loosen. In fact, the opposite will happen. Besides, the jar might burst if it warms up.
W3,2 = 'D'
St. Cold water cools the lid. It will contract and it will be even more difficult to unscrew than before.
I1,2
St. It has to consist of just one identification letter.

Example 14

The name of the instructional type is recorded *under* the sequence heading. The type name is followed by a semicolon and by the label 'A..D' which determines the *basic set*, i.e. the set of the *admissible* response indicators:

A, B, C, D.

The phrase **single selection** determines the I-dialogue element. It ensures that the answer is tested for inadmissibility and gets the corresponding feedback. The learner has to select exactly one of the admissible response indicators, hence *single* selection. If he or she fails to do so at the first time, he or she will receive the typological[1] comment:

(1) Unfortunately your answer is inadmissible. It has to consist of exactly one response indicator.

If the learner gives an inadmissible answer for the second time, the lesson will be finished with the following (typological) model comment:

(2) Unfortunately your answer is inadmissible. It has to consist of exactly one response indicator. The correct answer is: C.
Hot water warms up the lid. Since it consists of metal, it will expand and can therefore be screwed off more easily.

The typification "**Single Selection; A..D.**" determines the I-dialogue unequivocally. The specific high number h_I has the (typological) value 2 unless stated otherwise. For example, the expression

1 **Single Selection; A..D; h_I = 3.**

---

[1] *Typological* stands for *determined by the instructional type.*

would have the effect that comment (1) would also be given after the second inadmissible response. The learner would then receive the model comment only after his third inadmissible response.

As said above (in Chapter I on page 39), the overall high number h, which limits further the number of responses possible in a module (in addition to the specific high numbers), is noted down in the head. In the case h=4, we get the following expression in accordance with 1:

2   **Single Selection; A..D; h$_I$ = 3; h = 4.**

2. Head Structure
Each head, regardless of whether it is a hierarchy, a sequence or a module head, begins with the label of the unit in question.

a) *Sequence Head*
The sequence label is followed by the sequence heading, which may comprise several lines, at a horizontal distance of three spaces. The *main* sequence head is identical to the hierarchy head. However, the hea*ding* of the main sequence relates only to this main sequence but not to the whole hierarchy. As explained on pages 45 and 57 f., the sequence heading *always* contains a learner-oriented component (printed in *italics*); it may also contain methodical hints for the reader and critic (printed in roman).[1]

Apart from the sequence heading, the sequence head *may* contain strictly technical information determining the lesson. This technical head area could include the following: instructional type and type parameter; high numbers; sets and texts (and their names) needed in *several* modules of the sequence.[2] The technical area follows the heading (at the same column position) at a distance of one space line. If existing, the sequence lead-in (see page 45) will follow, which, together with the heading, forms the sequence theme.

The letter 'x' in Figure 20 (page 99) stands for the last sign of the sequence label. Thus, x is either a full stop in the case of a main sequence or a closing bracket.

---

[1] See the table of contents on page 152 in the Appendix.

[2] The technical area of the sequence head can also act as the *auxiliary section* for *module-transgressing* matters. See also page 119 (Point 7).

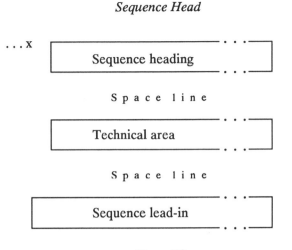

Figure 20

As for the validity of the objects defined in the technical area of the sequence head, we agree on the following:

(3) The instructional type given in the technical area of the sequence head applies to all modules of the sequence. However, it only concerns type *parameters* and high numbers if it does not contradict module-specific regulations. The texts and sets defined in the technical area can be referred to in any module of the sequence.

If a sequence type (an instructional type of a sequence) has been defined, module types (of the sequence in question) will be inadmissible. Texts and sets, however, can be additionally determined in the corresponding *modular auxiliary sections*.

b) *Module Head*

From what was stated above follows: 1) The head of the module does not contain any information about its content; the content of the module is summed up in the sequence theme. 2) An instructional type can only then be stated in the technical area of the module head if no instructional type has been specified in the sequence. Hence, if different instructional types are to be effective in one sequence, there can be no sequence type. *Modifications* to the sequence type such as module-specific parameters and high numbers are permitted.

3. Selection Indicators

One-place response indicators can be, for example, digits, but also small and capital letters. The definition of the response indicators which are *admissible* in a particular sequence or in a module follows the name of the instructional type, with the first and last digit or the first and last letter being specified. Thus, the set of capital letters A, B, C, and D is determined by the *definiens* 'A..D' (as in 1 of Point 1). If 'A..D' was replaced by the expression 'a..e', then the set B (basic set) of admissible response indicators would be a, b, c, d, e.

Many selection procedures require compound response indicators. Thus, the definiens 'A1..C3' determines

A1, A2, A3, B1, B2, B3, C1, C2, C3

as the admissible response indicators. It is quite obvious how this set is determined by 'A1..C3'. Set B can also be defined explicitly. If *several* response indicators separated by commas are given after the instructional type, then only they constitute the set of admissible response indicators. Some examples are given in the following table.

Definition of Sets of Admissible Response Indicators
Examples

Definiens Following the Instructional Type	Defined Response Indicators
A..C	A, B, C
1..11	1, 2, 3, 4, 5, 6, 7, 8, 9, 10, 11
A1..E3	A1, A2, A3, B1, B2, B3, C1, C2, C3, D1, D2, D3, E1, E2, E3
1A..2B	1A, 1B, 2A, 2B
G, H	G, H
3, 4, 7, 10	3, 4, 7, 10
C5, G1	C5, G1
C..E, G..J	C, D, E, G, H, I, J
1..3, 7..10	1, 2, 3, 7, 8, 9, 10
A..C, F..H, L, S, X, Z	A, B, C, F, G, H, L, S, X, Z

Table 6

Selection Types and Head Structure 101

4. Selection in a Narrower Sense

The following table shows the instructional types that refer to selections in a *narrower*[1] sense. The typological I-comments can be found in the last column. The variables (printed in bold) are explained further below.

Selection Types
and
Corresponding I-Comments

	Selection Type (Instructional Type)	Typological I-Comment (Interim *and* Final Comment)
a	**Free selection**	Unfortunately your answer is inadmissible. It may only contain response indicators, and each of them not more than once.
b	**Single selection**	Unfortunately your answer is inadmissible. It has to consist of exactly one response indicator.
c	**Double selection; triple selection;** ⋮	Unfortunately your answer is inadmissible. It has to consist of exactly **number** response indicators.
d	**Common selection**	Unfortunately your answer is inadmissible. It may only contain response indicators, and each of them not more than once. Each has to consist of **a starting sign** and **a finishing sign** (in this order). The response indicators have to be separated from each other by a comma, semicolon, or full stop.
e	**Double common selection; triple common selection;** ⋮	Unfortunately your answer is inadmissible. It has to consist of exactly **number** response indicators. Each has to consist of **a starting sign** and **a finishing sign** (in this order). The response indicators have to be separated from each other by a comma, semicolon, or full stop.

Table 7

---

[1] Selections in a *broader* sense may include matching (or other operations) of the selected indicators in addition to the selection. See § 13 (from page 103).

We have already discussed the instructional type (b). The types of the *multiple* "precise" selection are given under (c). The value of the variable **number** in the typological I-comment is determined by the corresponding type. Type (a) represents the *free* selection: the learner is allowed to answer with *any* non-empty subset of admissible response indicators. (Examples are given in the Appendix on pages 157 and 160.)

The response judging for (a), (b) and (c) is handled in a tolerant manner: the learner only needs to enter the response indicators. This implies:

(4)   When working with the types (a), (b), or (c), the author must use only *one-place* indicators for the designation of selection responses.

If compound indicators were to be admitted, the author would have to insist on the input of separating signs. The procedure according to (4), however, is very tolerant as to entering responses.

(5)   In answers corresponding to the instructional types (a), (b), or (c), the learner can enter spaces, commas, semicolons, parentheses and full stops but does not have to do so.

The **common selection** contains several questions concerning one and the same theme; each question can be answered with a free selection according to type (a). The common selection uses compound response indicators. They usually consist of one digit for the question and one letter for the selected response. All first and all second components of a module's response indicators must belong to the *same* elementary set *respectively*. The definiens '1A..3C' e.g. determines the basic set:

1A, 1B, 1C, 2A, 2B, 2C, 3A, 3B, 3C.

If the number of responses anticipated for different questions varies in size, the admissible indicators have to be stated separately for each question (see the examples on pages 156 and 161):

3   1A..1C, 2A..2B, 3A..3D, 4A..4B.

(The type parameters 3 are also noted after the type name, in our example after '**Common Selection**'.)

As for the I-comment of the instructional types (d) and (e) in Table 7, the value of the variable **starting sign** depends on what kind of sign the type parameter is. If, for example, the starting signs are digit strings, 'digit string' replaces the variable name '**starting sign**' in the given comment. By analogy, this is also true for the finishing sign.

§ 13 Matching

Matching is a form of selection in a broader sense. Objects are selected from at least two sets of objects — sentences, expressions, images etc. — *and* are matched with each other.[1] The response indicators of a matching module are compound or even *complex*. Table 8 shows sets of complex indicators and their definitions.

Complex Response Indicators

Type Parameter (Definiens)	$1\cdot1 .. 2\cdot3$	$(1;1) .. (2;2)$	$(0;1), (1;0)$	$A1\cdot B1 .. A2\cdot B3$
Pre-Image Set	1, 2	1, 2	0, 1	A1, A2
Image Set	1, 2, 3	1, 2	0, 1	B1, B2, B3
Set B of Admissible Response Indicators	$1\cdot1,\ 1\cdot2,$ $1\cdot3,\ 2\cdot1,$ $2\cdot2,\ 2\cdot3$	$(1;1),$ $(1;2), (2;1),$ $(2;2)$	$(0;1), (1;0)$	$A1\cdot B1,\ A1\cdot B2,$ $A1\cdot B3, A2\cdot B1,$ $A2\cdot B2,\ A2\cdot B3$

Table 8

Matching is usually not a symmetric procedure. In accordance with mathematical usage, we call the set of objects from which we proceed the *pre-image set*. The elements of the pre-image set are matched with those of the *image set*. The element of the pre-image set takes the first position of the type parameter. Thus the definiens '$1\cdot1 .. 2\cdot3$' contains '1' and '2' respectively in first position; it defines the pre-image set {1,2}. '1' and '3' respectively in the last position determine the image set {1,2,3}. Together with the multiplication sign, this yields the following set of admissible matching signs:

$$B = \{1\cdot1,\ 1\cdot2,\ 1\cdot3,\ 2\cdot1,\ 2\cdot2,\ 2\cdot3\}.$$

---

[1] The two-dimensional matching dealt with here is a special case of $(n+1)$-dimensional matching, which can be defined by analogy to the general notion of function. (The values of n independent quantities are matched with the dependent variable unequivocally, injectively, or bijectively.)

An example:

Matching with Complex Indicators[1]

002.   *Complementary Factors.*
        Unequivocal Matching; $1 \cdot 1 .. 6 \cdot 36$.

The integer 28 is divisible by six integers. These are called factors
of 28. The general rule is as follows:

> An integer b is called factor of an integer a if there is an
> integer c with
>
> $$a = b \cdot c.$$

For example, 4 is a factor of 28 because $4 \cdot 7 = 28$. This is also true
of the integer 7. There is a mutual relation between these two
factors:

$$28:4 = 7 \quad \text{and} \quad 28:7 = 4.$$

We call two factors of 28 that correlate in this way — whose
product is 28 — *complementary factors of 28.* We can now arrange
the factors of 28 in pairs, always combining complementary factors:
$1 \cdot 28; 2 \cdot 14; 4 \cdot 7$. The number of factors is in that case an even
integer: 6.
< key >

Find the complementary factors of 36 to the integers 1, 2, 3, 4, 6.
Write them in products

integer · complementary factor,

separating the products by commas.

Model answer: $1 \cdot 36, 2 \cdot 18, 3 \cdot 12, 4 \cdot 9, 6 \cdot 6$

R1,1 =   m = 5
P1,3 =   m > 0
        St. You did not find the correct complementary factors to the
        integers **S-first-element**.
W1,2
        St.

Example 15

---

[1] The notion **unequivocal matching** is explained on page 106. For the explanation of '< **key** >'
and of the following *clearing line*, see Appendix C, pages 163 f. The variable **S-first-element** is
explained in Point 5 of § 14 on page 117.

In the following we will distinguish four types of matching: **free matching, unequivocal matching, injective matching,** and **bijective matching.**

1. Free Matching[1]

accepts any non-empty subset of the set of admissible responses. The typological I-comment depends on the response indicators used. For *uncomplex* response indicators it reads:

(6)   Unfortunately your answer is inadmissible. It may only contain response indicators, and each of them not more than once. Each has to consist of one of the elements **of the pre-image set** and one of the elements **of the image set** (in this order). The response indicators must be separated from each other.

Both variables are determined by the type parameter. For example, if the type parameter is 'A1..D3', then

A, B, C or D

is substituted for '**of the pre-image set**' and

1, 2 or 3

for '**of the image set**' in the comment.

In the case of *complex* response indicators whose linking sign is not a semi-colon the last two sentences of (6) have to be replaced.

(7)   Unfortunately your answer is inadmissible. It may only contain response indicators, and each of them not more than once. Each has to consist of one of the elements **of the pre-image set**, a **linking sign**, and one of the elements **of the image set** (in this order).

The meaning of the variable **linking sign** is determined by the type parameter. If the linking sign is a semicolon, (7) is replaced by (8).

(8)   Unfortunately your answer is inadmissible. It may only contain response indicators, and each of them not more than once. Each has to consist of an opening parenthesis, one of the elements **of the pre-image set**, a semicolon, one of the elements **of the image set**, and a closing parenthesis (in this order).

---

[1] In the German edition this instructional type was simply called 'matching'.

2. Unequivocal Matching
requires that *each* element of the pre-image set is matched with *exactly one* element of the image set. Hence each element of the pre-image set must occur in exactly one response indicator. The following rectangular diagram illustrates the unequivocal matching.

Unequivocal Matching[1]

5			x	x
4				
3				
2	x			
1		x		
IS PS	1	2	3	4

Figure 21

The bottom line shows the response indicators of the pre-image set (PS): 1, 2, 3 and 4; the first vertical column shows those of the image set (IS): 1, 2, 3, 4 and 5. The crosses mark the locations of the right answers. Thus the correct response indicators are:

$$(1;2), (2;1), (3;5), (4;5).$$

(In the type **free matching** the squares of Figure 21 could be marked at will.) We get the typological I-comment of the **unequivocal matching** with the help of (7), adding the following.

(9)   Each of the elements **of the pre-image set** has to occur in the response (at the beginning of exactly one response indicator).

If the linking sign is a semicolon, the following has to be added to (8).

(10)   Each of the elements **of the pre-image set** has to occur in the response (immediately after the opening parenthesis of exactly one response indicator).

---

[1] For examples see pages 104, Example 15, and page 159.

3. Injective Matching[1]

further limits the number of admissible responses. A matching type is called injective firstly if it is unequivocal and secondly if each element of the image set occurs *at most* once. The "set of crosses" in Figure 22 reads

$$(1;1), (2;2), (3;5), (4;4).$$

Injective Matching

5			x	
4				x
3				
2		x		
1	x			
IS PS	1	2	3	4

Figure 22

In the case of response indicators without parentheses, the typological I-comment consists of (7), (9) and

(11) Each of the elements **of the image set** may occur at most once in the response (at the end of a response indicator).

In the case of *parenthesized* indicators it consists of (8), (10) and

(12) Each of the elements **of the image set** may occur at most once in the response (immediately before a closing parenthesis).

4. Bijective Matching

is firstly injective, and secondly, each sign of the image set occurs exactly once. In other words, each element of the pre-image set is matched with precisely one element of the image set and vice versa. Consequently, each row and each column of the matching diagram is occupied exactly once.

---

[1] For an example see page 116.

Bijective Matching

4		x		
3			x	
2	x			
1				x
IS PS	1	2	3	4

Figure 23

The set of crosses is:

(1;2), (2;4), (3;3), (4;1).

The typological I-comment consists of (7) and, in the case of response indicators without parentheses, (13).

(13)   Each of the elements **of the pre-image set** (at the beginning of the response indicator) and each of the elements **of the image set** (at the end) must occur exactly once.

In the case of parenthesized response indicators, (8) is supplemented by (14).

(14)   Each of the elements **of the pre-image set** (immediately after the opening parenthesis) and each of the elements **of the image set** (immediately before the closing parenthesis of a response indicator) must occur exactly once.

5. Succession[1]

requires that the response indicators are arranged in a particular order. The following example from English grammar deals with the position of the adverb in the sentence.

Succession

002.   *Position of the Adverb in English Sentences.*
        Succession; A..D.

        Make a sentence out of the following elements:

        A. we; B. our mistake; C. found; D. soon.

        Enter the letters in the correct order.

---

[1] The instructional type **succession** is a special case of **bijective matching.**

Addition: We soon found our mistake.

R1,1 = 'ADCB'

P1,3 = 'DACB' v 'ACBD'

Your response is not wrong but your word order is unusual. *Adverbs of indefinite time* and *adverbs of frequency* usually go before the verb.

W1,2 = 'ACDB'

St. This is a typically Germanic word order which is not possible in English. Adverbs are never placed between the verb and the object. *Adverbs of indefinite time* usually go before the verb. For example: she sometimes comes late. The verb *to be* is an *exception*: she is sometimes late.

W2,2

St.

Example 16

The head (including the type specification) of the example determines the four letters A, B, C and D as admissible response indicators and requires that the response consists exactly of these four letters. (Full stop, semicolon, comma and spaces are tolerated as is usual in the case of one-place response indicators.) Thus the example has 4! = 24 admissible responses or permutations, not counting the trivial tolerance variants. Furthermore the instructional type **succession** allows us to replace

Before('A', 'D', 'C', 'B')

with

'ADCB'

both for the partial and the equals key.

> *An instructional type can simplify representation not only by substitution (e.g. of the I-dialogue) but also by (re-) interpretation.*[1]

The I-comment belonging to the **succession**-type reads:

(15) Unfortunately your answer is inadmissible. It may only contain response indicators, and each of them exactly once.

---

[1] Interpretation is the more interesting way of simplifying representation.

§ 14 Set-Based Response Keys and Standard Dialogues

1. Set Keys

We normally use the signs B, S and $\underline{S}$ and their indexed variants to designate sets:

$$\underline{1} \qquad \begin{array}{l} B, B_1, B_2, B_3, \dots \; ; \\ S, S_1, S_2, S_3, \dots \; ; \\ \underline{S}, \underline{S}_1, \underline{S}_2, \underline{S}_3, \dots \; . \end{array}$$

In selection types, B is the (basic) set of the admissible[1], S the set of the correct and $\underline{S}$ the set of the incorrect response indicators:

$$\underline{2} \qquad\qquad B = S + \underline{S} \, .$$

The set of admissible response indicators equals the union of the set of correct and that of incorrect response indicators. (Besides, S and $\underline{S}$ are disjoint sets; they have no element in common.)

In the case of modules with standard dialogues, set S is defined in the head in addition to B. For example,

$$\underline{3} \qquad \textbf{Single Selection; } h_I = 3; \; h = 4; \; B: \; A..D; \; S: \; C.$$

determines the sets

$$\underline{4} \qquad\qquad B = \{A,B,C,D\}, \quad S = \{C\}.$$

Please note that the *names* of the sets are stated in the head. (If we left out the names, we would have to agree on the *position* of the set definiens *in addition*.) If B and S are given, $\underline{S}$ (according to $\underline{2}$ the difference set B - S) is also known.

To designate the *power* (the number of elements) of a *subset* of one of the sets $\underline{1}$ we use the signs:

$$\underline{5} \qquad \begin{array}{l} b, b_1, b_2, b_3, \dots \; ; \\ s, s_1, s_2, s_3, \dots \; ; \\ \underline{s}, \underline{s}_1, \underline{s}_2, \underline{s}_3, \dots \; . \end{array}$$

Thus, the following inequalities are valid:

$$(16) \qquad \begin{array}{l} 0 \le b \le |B| \, , \\ 0 \le s \le |S| \, , \\ 0 \le \underline{s} \le |\underline{S}| \, , \end{array}$$

with $|B|$, $|S|$ and $|\underline{S}|$ indicating the power of B, S, and $\underline{S}$.

---

[1] Set B of admissible response indicators does not necessarily have to equal the set of admissible *responses*. The latter is often a set of subsets of B.

Let us now proceed to the set key itself. The response key

<u>6</u>   : s=2

requires that the response contains exactly two (different) elements of set S. If

<u>7</u>   S = {A,B,C}

was the case, <u>6</u> would require that the response contains *either* A and B *or* A and C *or* B and C. The elementary equivalent of <u>6</u> reads:

<u>8</u>   : 'A'&'B' v 'A'&'C' v 'B'&'C'.

Instead of the term 'set key' it would be more appropriate to speak of the subset key: the key determines subsets (of a given set). The subset key

(17)   : s=x   with   x = 0,1,2,3,...,n;   n=|S|

requires that exactly x different elements (an x-subset) of S occur in the response. Key (17) includes as extremes the *empty* and *improper* subsets with x=0 or x=n. The elementary equivalent of (17) is an adjunction of $\binom{n}{x}$ conjunctions each of whose consists of x elements. The subset key replaces long expressions by short ones.

In contrast to the partial subset key (17), the equals key

(18)   = s=x   with   x = 1,2,3,...,n; n = |S|,

requires that the response contains exactly x different response indicators of set S *and nothing else*.

The partial adjunctive subset key with the kernel

(19) $Or(s=x_1, s=x_2, ..., s=x_d, ..., s=x_D)$

and with

$$x_d = 0,1,2,...,|S|; d = 1,2,3,...,D$$

requires that *either* exactly x_1 different *or* exactly x_2 different *or* exactly x_3 different ... *or* exactly x_D different elements of S are contained in the response. The equals key forbids the occurrence of elements not included in S. The keys with kernels of the kind

(20)   s<x;   s>x;   s $\neq$ x.

are special cases of (19).[1]

The conjunctive subset key relates to *different* sets. Read as a partial key, the kernel :

(21) $And(s_1=x_1, s_2=x_2, ..., s_k=x_k, ..., s_K=x_K)$

---

[1] Thus, s<x means the same as Or(s=0, s=1, s=2, ..., s=x-1).

with the condition

$$x_k = 0,1,2,...,|S_k|; \quad k = 1,2,3,...,K,$$

requires that exactly x_1 different elements of set S_1 *and* exactly x_2 different elements of set S_2 ... *and* exactly x_K different elements of set S_K occur in the response. Read as an equals key, (21) furthermore requires that elements not contained in any of the sets S_1 to S_K may not occur in the response.

2. Rough-Standard Dialogue
The names of the rough-standard types consist of the names of the basic type in question (see §§ 12 and 13) and the addition '**rough standard**'. The rough standard indicates *only* whether the answer is right, wrong or inadmissible. The *full* designation of the instructional types consists of (see 3 on page 110):

(22)   Instructional type; I-high number h_I; overall high number h; B; S.

As has been said before, B stands for the set of admissible, S for the set of correct response indicators. The difference set[1] $\underline{S}$ of incorrect response indicators can be found on the basis of B and S.

Rough-Standard Selection Types[2]

Single selection, rough standard.
Double selection, rough standard.
Triple selection, rough standard.
. . .
. . .
. . .

Free selection, rough standard.
Common selection, rough standard.
Double common selection, rough standard.
Triple common selection, rough standard.
. . .
. . .
. . .

Free matching, rough standard.
Unequivocal matching, rough standard.
Injective matching, rough standard.
Bijective matching, rough standard.
Succession, rough standard.

Table 9

---

[1] $\underline{S}$ = B-S.
[2] The term 'selection' is used in the *broader* sense here.

The standard dialogues listed in Table 9 are determined in the following way:

Dialogues of the Selection Types with Rough Standard

Response Key	Interim Comment	Final Comment
I	See §§ 12 and 13.	
R = $\quad$ s = $|S|$	------	Correct! **Addition**
P: $\quad$ s > 0	Unfortunately your response is only partially correct.	Unfortunately your response is only partially correct. The correct response reads: **Model answer Addition**
W	Unfortunately the response indicators given are wrong.	Unfortunately your response is wrong. The correct response reads: **Model answer Addition**

Table 10

Comments on the Table 10:

a) The I-comments are the only ones (see §§ 12 and 13) that exclusively depend on the corresponding type. The comments of admissible responses depend only on the elements from S and $\underline{S}$ contained in them.

b) The model answer of the standard dialogues belonging to the selection types is determined by set S (see (22)) defined in the head.

$$(23) \qquad \text{If the elements of S are given in the order}$$
$$J_1, J_2, J_3, ..., J_n,$$
$$\text{the model answer reads}$$
$$J_1, J_2, J_3, ..., J_{n-1} \text{ ' and ' } J_n.$$

c) Note that the key-column reflects the *order of response judging*. I-judging takes place first, followed by R-, P- and W-judging. The P- and W-keys read:

$$(24) \qquad\qquad\qquad P: \ s > 0 \ \& \ \underline{s} \geq 0;$$

$$(25) \qquad\qquad\qquad W: \ s = 0 \ \& \ \underline{s} > 0.$$

The P-key is empty in the type **single selection**. The number of admissible response indicators $b = s + \underline{s}$ equals 1. It is not possible that both s and $\underline{s}$ are greater than zero; hence, there is no P-comment.

d) The I-interim comment is outputted as long as

$$a_I < h_I \quad and \quad a < h$$

are the case. The maximum frequency of P- and W-interim comments, however, is exclusively determined by

$$a < h.$$

3. Frequency Standard and Dialogue Variable

The type names can be obtained from Table 9 by substituting '**frequency standard**' for '**rough standard**'. The frequency standard informs us about the number of correct and incorrect signs and is therefore meaningless for the type **single selection**. Neither do frequencies play a part in I-, R- and W-dialogue elements: the corresponding comments are identical to those of the rough standard. The P-comments belonging to the frequency standard for $\underline{s} > 0$ can be obtained from the P-comments in Table 10 by adding the following sentence characteristic for the frequency standard:

(26)   You have given s correct and $\underline{s}$ incorrect response indicators.

after each first sentence. Note that s only counts *different* response indicators, as does $\underline{s}$. In the case of $\underline{s} = 0$, (26) is replaced by:

(27)   The response indicators given are correct but some are missing.

This comment can only occur with the types **free selection, common selection** and **free matching**. For all other instructional types of Table 9, $\underline{s} = 0$ implies that the response is either correct or inadmissible.

Response-dependent dialogue variables are introduced in (26). To be precise, we should not speak of comments but of *dialogue patterns*. Their manifoldness is determined by the ranges of their variables. Pattern (26), for example, determines up to

$$|S| \cdot |\underline{S}|$$

different dialogue elements. The corresponding key (24) only determines the frame but not the single dialogue elements. The dialogue variable in the *comment* does not only account for the fine structure of this comment but also of the corresponding key. The dialogue variables s and $\underline{s}$ have the effect that each value pair (s, $\underline{s}$) of (24) determines a key of its own. Thus the dialogue variable is an effective means of abbreviation.

4. Fine Standard

Although standardized, feedback by means of sets and their elements can be very informative. Whereas the P-comment of the frequency standard shows only *how many* response indicators are correct or incorrect, the fine standard also reveals *which* of the indicators given in the response are correct or incorrect. The names of the different selection types can again be obtained from Table 9 by replacing '**rough standard**' with '**fine standard**'. The *complete* labeling of the different types takes place according to (22).

The I-, R- and W-dialogue elements result from Table 10. The P-comments are summarized in the following:

P-Comments
of the
Fine Standard of Selection

	$\underline{s} = 0$	$\underline{s} > 0$
Interim Comment	Unfortunately your answer is only partially right. The given response indicators are correct but not complete.	Unfortunately your answer is only partially right. The response **indicator/indicators S-element is/are** correct but the **indicator/indicators S-element is/are** incorrect.
Final Comment	Unfortunately your answer is only partially right. The response indicators given are correct but not complete. The right answer is: **Model answer Addition**	Unfortunately your answer is only partially right. The response **indicator/indicators S-element is/are** correct but the **indicator/indicators S-element is/are** incorrect The right answer is: **Model answer Addition**

Table 11

In the corresponding comments, the dialogue variables **S-element** and **$\underline{S}$-element** are replaced by the correct indicators from S and the incorrect indicators from $\underline{S}$ respectively contained in the learner's response. If, for example, B is 'A1..D3' and S consists of the elements A2, B1, C3 and D1, then the learner's response

$$A1, B1, C2, D3$$

leads to the following output values

$$\textbf{S-element} = \text{'B1'}$$

and

$$\underline{\textbf{S}}\textbf{-element} = \text{'A1, C2 and D3.'}$$

The set elements will be given in their "natural" order[1]; between the last but one and the last element stands 'and'.

5. The Variable First-Element
Set keys and set-element variables do not only occur in pre-defined dialogues. These concepts can be applied whenever the corresponding sets are defined. This shall be illustrated in the following example (see also Appendix A, Hierarchy 004 on page 155):

First-Element

004.   *Experiment to Determine the Dependence of Water Pressure on the Immersion Depth.*
        Injective Matching; A1..G23.

How does the pressure change when the measuring tin is immersed increasingly deeper? Determine the pressure for 2 cm, 4 cm, 6 cm, 8 cm, 10 cm, 15 cm and 20 cm depth and indicate the corresponding interval. Enter your response in the following way: first enter the *identification letter* of the measurement and then the *number* of the corresponding interval.

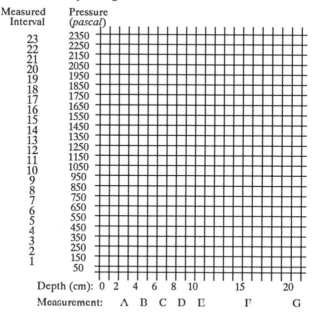

---

[1] A compound element J is "earlier" than J' if the pre-image component of J — in our example the capital letter — comes earlier in the alphabet than that of J'. If the pre-image components are the same, then the image component of the set element decides on the order.

Model answer: A2, B4, C6, D8, E10, F15, G20.

R1,1= s=7
    St. Well done! You have experimented very carefully!
P1,3: s>0
    St. The **result/results** of the measurement **S-first-element**
    is/are right but **that/those** of the measurements of **S̲-first-
    element is/are** incorrect.
W1,3
    C1 St. Are you sure that you have adjusted the depth correctly?
        Remember that the distance between the membrane of the
        measuring tin and the water surface is important! Or perhaps
        you are reading the pressure from the wrong arm of the U-
        manometer?
    C2 St. Check your measuring equipment. Does the U-manometer
        really read 0 Pa pressure when the tin has not been
        immersed? Check by shaking whether water has entered the
        measuring tin.

Example 17

Example 17 shows: 1) In the case of selection types with exclusively individual (not standardized) feedback, set S of correct response indicators is determined in the *auxiliary section*; 2) If set S is identical to the model answer, it will be noted down after '**model answer:**'.[1] The variables **S-first-element** and **S̲-first-element** are new in Example 17. The word 'first' stands for the *first* component of the response indicator.

(28)   The variables **S-first-element** and **S̲-first-element** indicate the *first* components of the (compound) elements of S and S̲ given in the learner's response.

If the learner fulfills the P1-requirement and answers e.g. with A1, B4, C5, D9, E10, F15 and G20, the elements B, E, F and G substitute for **S-first-element** and the elements A, C and D substitute for **S̲-first-element** in the comment. The advantage of this variable as opposed to the *general* set-element characterizations is that the comment can be better represented linguistically. If '**S̲-element**' replaced '**S̲-first-element**' in the P1-comment, it would read like this, "Unfortunately the response indicators **S̲-element** are incorrect." This would be a rather dull and stereotyped statement.

The use of the first-element variable is only possible in *unequivocal* matching. Only in this case does the admissibility testing ensure that each first

---

[1] Compare the reverse procedure in the case of standard types (page 113, expression (23)).

element, i.e. each element of the pre-image set, occurs exactly once. (In the case of the instructional type **free matching**, each first element could be part of *both* correct *and* incorrect response indicators. **S-first-element** and **S̲-first-element** could take on the same values.)

6. Notes on the Construction of Free-Response Types

Let us begin with an example.

Free-Response Module

02.   **h=6**

Name the four Gospels.

S: ' Matthew ', ' Mark ', ' John ', ' Luke'.

R1 : s=4
P1 : s=3
        St. You have named 3 Gospels.
P2 : s=2
        St. You have named 2 Gospels.
P3 : s=1
        St. You have named 1 Gospel.
U
        St. You have not named any Gospel.

Example 18

This module can be easily subsumed under a *general frequency standard*. We only need to introduce a *name* for set S, both in the singular and the plural:

Free-Response Frequency-Standard Example

02.   **Free Response, Frequency Standard; h=6.**

Name the four Gospels.

S-name: Gospel, Gospels.
S: ' Matthew ', ' Mark ', ' John ', ' Luke'.

Example 19

The standard dialogue of the instructional type is defined in accordance with Example 18 and with the help of Table 12 (see next page). The R-final comments are model comments. The model answer is determined by S according to (23) on page 113. However, the auxiliary section of the module might include a *specific* model answer (and naturally also an addition).

Free-Response Frequency Standard

R1 : $s = |S|$	**Model Comment**
P1 : $s > 1$	St. You have entered s **S-name**.
P2 : $s = 1$	St. You have entered 1 **S-name**.
U	Your answer is not correct. You have not entered any **S-name**.

Table 12

Practical free-response types will, in general, be based on *several* sets. (Apart from the "correct" set S an "inadmissible" set can be introduced containing, e.g., negative expressions such as 'not', 'none', 'either' etc. Thus a limited free-response type can be determined. Responses containing negations could immediately be classed as inadmissible. This would diminish the risk of an incorrect evaluation.[1])

7. Abbreviations

If texts occur *several times*, they can be abbreviated by *text, text 1, text 2* etc. If the text has a specific meaning, the author can use expressions such as

fact; observation; conclusion; definition; rule; principle; law; note; help; . . .

or others (with or without postpositive digits or letters). We agree on:

Text abbreviations are introduced
— in the auxiliary section of the module if they are used only in the corresponding module;
— in the technical area of the sequence head if they concern several modules of the corresponding sequence;
(29) — in the hierarchy head if they are used in the main sequence and/or in several sequences of the corresponding hierarchy;
— in the lead-in to the instrugram if they are used in several hierarchies *and* if they have superior didactic significance. (Whether a text abbreviation is noted down (several times) in several hierarchy heads or (once) in the lead-in to the instrugram depends on what the author thinks best suited.)

The names of the model answer and addition, i.e. '**Model answer**' and '**Addition**', introduced in the auxiliary section can also serve as abbreviations within their own modules.

---

[1] See page 6 of the Introduction.

Chapter V

TRACING BACK THE CALCULATION PATH

Calculation path tracing has greater significance than the instructional types discussed in the last chapter. Backward calculation path tracing shows that methods common to school teaching can be made more precise and complete with the help of Instruction Language. The algorithm underlying this instructional type is derived from the common practice of correcting mathematical calculations starting from the end with the solution. Even so, the instructional type discussed here has very little to do with correction needs. I believe that it has become a useful *algorithm for practice, diagnosis* and *therapy*. Perhaps the calculation path tracing method will be an incentive to objectify other and more interesting teaching methods.

OUTLINE:
The difference between judging syntax (form) and judging numerical value is discussed in § 15. The former concerns correct "mathematical spelling", and the latter is based on the fact that syntactically correct (mathematical) expressions have at least one numerical value. Correct syntax and correct numerical value are indispensable preconditions for *instructional* correctness. (It is emphasized that *factual* correctness is not necessary for instructional correctness.) Finally, the concepts of response step and calculation path are intro-

duced in the same paragraph. In §§ 16 and 17 an example of calculation path tracing is demonstrated in detail, and the general flowchart represented on pages 134 f. is explained. The difference between *response step*, *response* and *response sequence* is discussed in Point 2 of § 17. § 18 features the hybrid representation: the concurring combination of standardized (typologically predefined) dialogue with individual dialogue elements (or merely parts of those) written in elementary notation. The hybrid representation is an important instrument in optimizing readability, testability and improvability of instruction: only the particular is explicitly written down whereas anything that follows general patterns will be abbreviated by the corresponding instructional type. The procedure of answer judging in the hybrid module derives from the natural fact that whatever has been specially noted must not have been written down in vain.

§ 15 Syntax, Value and Response Step

In the entering and judging of mathematical responses we should note that mathematical expressions can firstly be *two-dimensional* in structure, that secondly they possess a *numerical value*, and that it can thirdly be useful to judge the response in a *sequence of response steps*.

While verbal expressions are usually one-dimensional (constructed by concatenation), mathematical expressions are very often two-dimensional. Individual signs are connected not only by joining them in a row, but also by placing them one below the other. The elementary two-dimensional form of expression that is most important is the fraction. Anyone who has tried to type fractions on a typewriter knows how troublesome that is. Without suitable assistance, teaching mathematics via the computer would fail only because of the problem of entering the response. The most obvious solution is to use the computer also as writing aid. But one has to be careful not to help "too much". The entering help should be neutral as regards instruction. However, computer science and programming need not take this into account as long as they are not used in *instruction*. Mathematics is *applied* in technology and economy in *linearized*[1] form — by the expert. (This is due to the programming languages used in these fields, such as FORTRAN.)

---

[1] In the early stages of calculation teaching, the (horizontal) fraction bar can be replaced by a slash, if need be. This is, however, not possible in a *systematic* course on calculating fractions.

1. Judging Syntax and Numerical Value

We test *verbal* answers exclusively on whether they have the required form of *representation*. If yes, we say that the answer was *right*. But we have to be careful. The statements "The answer is right in terms of the instrugram" or "The answer is R-right" would be more precise. However, the first expression is too long, and the second too technical. It is better to say the answer is *instructionally right*. By analogy, we use the expressions 'partly instructionally right', 'instructionally wrong', etc. Mathematical answers can be judged far more rigorously than verbal answers. First of all, we can check whether their *form* is correct, i.e. whether they comply with the rules of mathematical *syntax*. For example,

$$4 + \cdot \ 3$$

is syntactically wrong. We realize at once, without having to consult the instrugram, that such a response cannot be *instructionally correct*.

The numerical *value* of a mathematical sign can also be checked regardless of the response criteria given in the instrugram. For example, if 50 : 5 is to be calculated and the learner enters 1 as the answer, the answer is syntactically correct, since 1 is a number; the answer, however, is numerically wrong, since the correct number has the value 10. Syntactically *and* numerically correct would be the answer 20 : 2 . However, this answer is instructionally wrong, since the instrugram asks for the numeral '10'. We now have three different concepts of what 'correct' may mean:

syntactically correct, numerically correct and *instructionally correct*.

Sometimes we also have to differentiate between *instructionally* and *factually correct*. What is instructionally correct need not be factually correct. The reason for this is that learning is a step-by-step process, and that factual correctness is one of the *last* steps in this process.[1]

Correct numerical value is necessary for a mathematical answer to be instructionally correct: if the answer does not have the correct numerical *value*, then it cannot be instructionally correct. For an answer to be numerically correct requires in turn that it be syntactically correct; a syntactically wrong answer has no determinable value and is useless.

Since both judging syntax and numerical value are independent of the specific lesson, they can be carried out by a *general* program in accordance with an equally universal algorithm, before the "instruction-logical" judging (which is done according to the specific instrugram). The general program has to ensure that the learner can use the same form of writing which he

---

[1] The term *step* is used here in its general meaning. It has nothing to do with the formal concept of step discussed in the next number.

would normally use in school. It can also check the syntax of the calculation and comment on mistakes like the following:

— The numerical value of the denominator is zero;
— Several arithmetic symbols follow immediately one after the other;
— The term begins with a multiplication sign;
— The term begins with a division sign;
— The term ends with an arithmetic sign;
— There is no arithmetic sign between two fractions;
— The term includes a forbidden sign.

If the syntax is correct, the program checks whether the term is numerically correct. If the learner has neither responded instructionally correctly, nor made mistakes anticipated by the instrugrammer, he can at least be told whether his calculations have the correct numerical value.

2. Calculation Path and Calculation Steps

A calculation path is a sequence of calculation *steps*. A calculation step contains precisely one equals sign (it is, at most, one line long) and is marked by a number in brackets; this number is placed at the beginning of the calculation line. If the calculation step is a term, the equals sign follows the bracketed step number.

Calculation Path

$$4\frac{1}{2} : 3\frac{3}{4}$$ Problem

$$[1] \quad = \frac{9}{2} : \frac{15}{4}$$ First calculation step

$$[2] \quad = \frac{6}{5}$$ Second calculation step

$$[3] \quad - 1\frac{1}{5}$$ Third calculation step

Example 20

The vertical arrangement of the calculation has *methodical* reasons: transformations of *terms* and those of *equations*, which have exactly one equals sign in the "middle" of the calculation line, have to be clearly differentiated.

The interplay of input and output: the learner is given the problem (of Example 20) on the screen as well as the number [1] and the equals sign printed at the beginning of the first calculation line. The computer then waits for a response. When the learner has finished the first calculation step, he must tell the computer. If, say, the learner has entered the expression of the first *calculation line* of Example 20 (and if he has told the computer that he has finished the line), the machine then prints the number [2] and the equals sign of the second calculation line, asking the learner for another (partial) response. After entering the third (last) step, the learner has to signalize not only the end of this step but also that of the whole calculation path, i.e. of the complete response.

§ 16 Tracing Back the Calculation Path — Concept and Example

The learner's way of solving an arithmetic problem is examined from the bottom to the top, that is, starting with the solution at the end and moving backwards (hence "tracing *back* the calculation path"). When a teacher corrects a math test, he usually does the same: he begins at the end of each calculation. The basic principle of calculation path tracing is to search for an *instructionally correct* calculation step, i.e. a step which, in the opinion of the instrugrammer, should be part of the calculation. The search begins at the last step and, if the result is negative, goes back step by step so as to find an instructionally correct interim step. If such an interim step is found, the learner will be told a) that his calculation was correct up to this point, and b) *which mistake he made after this step*. He is then asked to calculate again, starting this time from the correct interim step.

The success of this method depends on whether the author has anticipated the relevant correct and incorrect steps and has included them in his instrugram. If this demand seems unrealistic, it should be considered that instrugramming is designed for *empiric testability*: it is not the *immediate success* which counts but the possibility of improvement and the actual, *successive improvement* of instruction.[1]

---

[1] First instruction sketches will not be satisfactory, and later ones not good enough: we are looking for ways and methods which help us to recognize our mistakes better.

1. Introductory Example

Calculation Path Tracing

078.   *Dividing Mixed[1] Numbers.*
       Backward Calculation Path Tracing ; min=3; h$_{min}$=3.

Show what you have learned by solving the following problem.

$$4\tfrac{1}{2} : 3\tfrac{3}{4}$$

Enter the complete calculation.

Model Answer		**Error Survey**		
$4\tfrac{1}{2}:3\tfrac{3}{4}$		1	2	3
T1 $= \dfrac{9}{2}:\dfrac{15}{4}$		$\dfrac{*}{2}:\dfrac{*}{4}$	$\dfrac{*}{2}:(3\tfrac{3}{4} \text{ v } \tfrac{15}{4})$	$(4\tfrac{1}{2} \text{ v } \tfrac{9}{2}):\dfrac{*}{4}$
T2 $= \dfrac{9}{2}\cdot\dfrac{4}{15}$		$\dfrac{2}{9}\cdot\dfrac{4}{15}$	$\dfrac{2}{9}\cdot\dfrac{15}{4}$	$\dfrac{135}{8} \text{ v } 16\tfrac{7}{8}$
$= \dfrac{9\cdot4}{2\cdot15}$				
T3 $= \dfrac{3\cdot2}{1\cdot5}$		$\dfrac{*\cdot2}{1\cdot*}$	$\dfrac{3\cdot*}{*\cdot5}$	$\dfrac{36}{30}$
T4 $= \dfrac{6}{5}$		$\dfrac{*}{5}$	$\dfrac{6}{*}$	
T5 $= 1\tfrac{1}{5}$		$*\tfrac{1}{5}$	$\tfrac{1}{5}$	

---

[1] We are not going to discuss the terminological confusion about the difference between *number* and *numeral*, which is so dominant in mathematics. On the one hand people talk about improper fractions, with 'fraction' referring to an expression, while 'improper' refers to a number property. The opposite is true for the term 'mixed number': strangely enough, the word 'number' refers here to an *expression* which has a mixed form. (See Quine (1951), p. 23.)

R01,1 T_5

R02,2 $T_5 T_0$
St.

R03,3 $T_5 F_0$
St.

P01,2 $T_4 F_{5;1}$
StT. The value of your result, however, is not equal to the value of [t]. You made a mistake in changing the fraction to a mixed number. The integer of your mixed number is wrong.

P02,2 $T_4 F_{5;2}$
StT. But $\frac{6}{5} = \frac{1}{5}$ cannot be true, can it? After changing the improper fraction to a mixed number, you have forgotten to note down the integer of the mixed number.

P03,3 $T_4 F_0$
C1 StT. After this step, there is a mistake in your calculation. Try to find your mistake.
C2 You should be able to change an improper fraction to a mixed number. I will give you an example:

$$\frac{3}{2} = \frac{2}{2} + \frac{1}{2}$$
$$= 1 + \frac{1}{2}$$
$$= 1\frac{1}{2}$$

Now change the fraction [t] to a mixed number in the same way and enter the correct result.

P04,3 $T_4 T_0$
StT. But the final result is missing.

P05,2 T_4
Fraction [t] is not the final result. The final result has to be either an integer, a proper fraction, or a mixed number. It can never be an improper fraction.

P06,3 $T_3 F_{4;1}$
StT. You made a mistake while calculating $3 \cdot 2$. Correct the mistake and complete the exercise.

P07,3 $T_3 F_{4;2}$
StT. You made a mistake in calculating $1 \cdot 5$. Correct your mistake and complete the exercise.

P08,3 $T_3 F_0$
StT. What did you do after that? Check whether you have multiplied correctly. What are $3 \cdot 2$ and $1 \cdot 5$?

P09,3 $T_3 F_0$
StT. But the final result is missing.

P10,2 T_3

You have not completed your calculation. Go on calculating with [t].

P11,3 $T_2F_{3;1}$

C1 StT. You reduced the fraction correctly (dividing both numerator and denominator by 2). You have also realized that it can be reduced once more. In doing so, however, you made a mistake. Try to find your mistake and correct it.

C2 Unfortunately you have not found your mistake. Fraction [t] can be reduced by 3. Divide 9 and 15 each by 3. Enter the fraction reduced to its lowest terms, and then go on with your calculation.

P12,3 $T_2F_{3;2}$

C1 You reduced fraction [t] correctly, dividing both numerator and denominator by 3. Then you reduced the fraction again but made a mistake. Try to find your mistake and correct it.

C2 Unfortunately you have not found your mistake. Fraction [t] can also be reduced by 2. Divide both 4 and 2 by 2 and enter the correct result. Then go on with your calculation.

P13,2 $T_2F_{3;3}$

You forgot to reduce the fraction [t] to its lowest terms. Remember, always reduce fractions to their lowest terms before multiplying.

P14,3 T_2F_0

StT. You made a mistake. Did you check whether the fractions could be reduced before multiplying?

P15,3 T_2T_0

StT But the final result is missing.

P16,2 T_2

You have not completed your calculation.

P17,2 $T_1F_{2;1}$

You changed the two mixed numbers to improper fractions correctly. But you seem to have forgotten how to divide by a fraction. Only the fraction by which you are dividing has to be inverted. But you inverted both fractions!

P18,2 $T_1F_{2;2}$

StT. But you inverted the dividend (the fraction *in front* of the division sign) instead of the divisor (the fraction after the division sign). To divide by a fraction, multiply by the reciprocal of the fraction. The first fraction remains unchanged.

P19,2 $T_1F_{2;3}$

StT. You just multiplied the fractions. But you are supposed to divide by $\frac{15}{4}$.

P20,3 T_1F_0
C1 StT. Then you made a mistake. Can you find it?
C2 Unfortunately you haven't found your mistake. How do we divide by a fraction? Have you forgotten? To divide by a fraction, multiply by the reciprocal of the fraction. Did you pay attention to that?

P21,3 T_1T_0
StT. But the final result is missing.

P22,2 T_1
You have not completed your calculation.

W01,3 $F_{1;1}$
C1 StF. You transformed the mixed numbers incorrectly. Try to find your mistake.
C2 Unfortunately this is still wrong. Have you forgotten how to change mixed numbers to improper fractions? I'll show you how to do it by giving you an example:

$$2\frac{1}{3} = 2 + \frac{1}{3}$$
$$= \frac{6}{3} + \frac{1}{3}$$
$$= \frac{7}{3}$$

Now change the mixed numbers in the exercise to fractions the same way.
C3 Unfortunately this is wrong again. You have to practice changing mixed numbers to fractions.
Hierarchy 16-19

W02,3 $F_{1;2}$
C1 You made a mistake in changing the mixed number $4\frac{1}{2}$ to an improper fraction. Try again.
C2 This is still wrong. Correct is:

$$4\frac{1}{2} = 4 + \frac{1}{2}$$
$$= \frac{8}{2} + \frac{1}{2}$$

Go on with this calculation.

W03,3 $F_{1;3}$
C1 You changed the term behind the division sign incorrectly. Correct your mistake.
C2 Unfortunately this is still wrong. Correct is:

$$3\frac{3}{4} = 3 + \frac{3}{4}$$
$$= \frac{12}{4} + \frac{3}{4}$$

Go on with this calculation.

UT ,3 T_0
The final result is missing.

UF ,3

    C1 Check your calculation. First you have to change the mixed numbers to improper fractions.

    C2 Did you transform the mixed numbers correctly? You can then write the problem as a division problem with improper fractions. Go on with the calculation and enter it step by step.

Example 21

2. Comments

min stands for minimum. The minimum condition **min = 3** requires that *at least one* of the learner's responses should consist of *at least three* response steps. If this is not the case, his response will not be accepted. The high number $h_{min} = 3$ limits the number of such responses: $h_{min} = 3$ has the effect that a final comment is given after the third "miniresponse". (For further information on commenting see § 18 on page 138 ff.)

The **model answer** given in the auxiliary section contains the model calculation. T_1 to T_5 (t: true) are the response steps, which — beginning with T_5 — are looked for in the learner's calculation. (The unmarked step between T_2 and T_3 is printed in the final comments, but is irrelevant for calculation path tracing.) Mistakes are printed next to the corresponding T-steps in the error survey of the auxiliary section. The mistakes (f: false)

$$F_{1;1} = \frac{*}{2} : \frac{*}{4} \qquad F_{1;2} = \frac{*}{2} : (3\frac{3}{4} \text{ v } \frac{15}{4}) \qquad F_{1;3} = (4\frac{1}{2} \text{ v } \frac{9}{2}) : \frac{*}{4}$$

belong to the response step

$$T_1 = \frac{9}{2} : \frac{15}{4}.$$

$F_{1;1}$ refers to all products (containing no mixed numbers) in which the first asterisk represents any expression other than '9' and/or the second asterisk any expression other than '15'. $F_{1;2}$ and $F_{1;3}$ stand for mistakes in the numerator of the first or second fraction respectively (allowing, however, the corresponding mixed number in place of the "correct" fraction). The mistakes $F_{2;1}$, $F_{2;2}$ and $F_{2;3}$ belong to response step T_2, and so on.

This relationship between model calculation and mistake spectrum (error survey) is based on the idea that if the learner's answer contains the T_r-step but not the T_{r+1}-step, the learner must have made a F_{r+1}-mistake (a mistake of the kind $F_{r+1;1}$, $F_{r+1;2}$, ...). If, for example, the model step

$$T_4 = \frac{6}{5}$$

is contained in the learner's response, and the solution

$$T_5 = 1\frac{1}{5}$$

is not, then it is assumed that one of the mistakes

$$F_{5;1} = * \frac{1}{5} \quad \text{or} \quad F_{5;2} = \frac{1}{5}$$

was made: the instrugrammer has anticipated the comments that are necessary for this situation in the instrugram. Hence, if a F_5-mistake occurs, the learner can be helped very easily. *Searching for and correction of mistakes proceed directly from what the learner can do.* I believe that this is an important characteristic of relevant practice.[1]

As for the answer keys of Example 21, the type **Backward Calculation Path Tracing** substitutes missing logical connections and elementary Instruction Language symbols and expressions. This instructional type attributes the following meaning to (for example)

$$T_4 F_{5;1}:$$

a P01-answer is an answer which *contains* one step that *equals*[2] T_4, and another *later* step which equals $F_{5;1}$.

The R01-answer is the answer the instrugrammer wants. It is given if the *last* answer step entered by the learner is the solution and if at least two steps have been entered previously, as required by the minimum condition discussed above. The R02-answer contains the required solution T_5, but *after* it, at least one step with *correct numerical value* has been entered. (For further details of feedback, see § 18 on page 138 ff.) The R03-answer also contains the solution T_5, but again the learner went on calculating, and gave a *numerically wrong* answer in the last step. Answer attributes with *correct* or *incorrect numerical value*, indicated by T_0 or F_0 respectively, are called UT or UF. These attributes are given to those answers which belong to none of the *previous* attributes (and which have correct or incorrect numerical value).

The variable **t** appears for the first time in the P01-comment. The computer replaces **t** with the *number of the calculation step* which has been assigned to the T-step found by the learner. In the P01-comment this is the number in front of the entered step

$$\frac{6}{5}.$$

---

[1] One of my students, Stefan Langsdorf, has suggested to generalize the search for and the correction of mistakes as follows: in case of a T_r-step the learner's answer is to be tested not only for an F_{r+1}-mistake but also for F_{r+2}-, F_{r+3}-, F_{r+4}-mistakes, etc., which are included in the error survey. Obviously, having entered, for example, the T_2-step, the learner might try to enter the final solution T_5 at once, but makes an F_5-mistake. (The flowchart represented on pages 134 f. can be generalized accordingly without problems.)

[2] Except for missing or additional spaces. (Note that the number of fraction bars must not be changed.)

We will take a closer look at the step number variable in the next paragraph.
The standard comments indicated by

St; StT; StF

will be discussed in § 18, Point 2 (pages 139 ff.).

§ 17 The Flow of Instruction and the Notion of Response Step

1. Comments on the Flowchart of Calculation Path Tracing
We will now discuss the flowchart depicted on pages 134 f.

The overall answer counter a counts all answers except those which are syntactically wrong.

$$a = a_{min} + a_{n,0} + a_{n,-1} + a_{n,-2} + \Sigma a_{r,0} + \Sigma\Sigma a_{rk} + \Sigma a_{r,-1} + \Sigma a_{r,-2} + \Sigma\Sigma a'_{wk} + a_{0,-1} + a_{0,-2}.$$

Thus, a counts a total of 11 types of responses: miniresponse; T_n; $T_n T_0$; $T_n F_0$; T_r; $T_r F_{r+1,k}$; $T_r T_0$; $T_r F_0$; $F_{w,k}$; T_0 and F_0.

a) a_{min} counts the miniresponses, i.e. the responses which are too short: they contain too few response steps.

b) $a_{n,0}$ "counts" the T_n-answer, i.e. the answer the instrugrammer was looking for. (In Example 21 this is: $1\frac{1}{5}$.)

c) $a_{n,-1}$ counts the $T_n T_0$-answers: the learner gave the correct answer but went on calculating *numerically correctly*.

d) $a_{n,-2}$ counts the $T_n F_0$-answers: having given the correct answer T_n, the learner went on calculating and made a *numerical* mistake in the *last* response step. (It will be explained below why this is the *last* step.)

e) $a_{r,0}$ counts the T_r-answers. They include only the non-last model answer step T_r.

f) a_{rk} counts the type of answers most important for calculation path tracing: $T_r F_{r+1,k}$. The answer includes a T_r-model answer step and a mistake, which *explains* why T_{r+1} is missing.

g) $a_{r,-1}$ counts the $T_r T_0$-answers. They include the non-last model answer step T_r and further numerically correct steps (but not the solution).

h) $a_{r,-2}$ counts the $T_r F_0$-answers: there is a non-last model answer step T_r; the last step is numerically wrong.

i) a'_{wk} counts the $F_{w,k}$-answers. They do not include a T_r-step but an expected $F_{w,k}$-mistake.

j) $a_{0,-1}$ counts the T_0-answers: answers which include neither a T- nor a F-step but which are numerically correct.

k) $a_{0,-2}$ counts the F_0-answers. Again, these include neither a T- nor a F-step, but the last step entered is numerically wrong.

All of these specific response counters have the value zero if the overall response counter is zero. (If a sum of non-negative addends has the value zero, then each of the addends has the value zero.) Thus, the initial condition

$$a \Leftarrow 0$$

also sets the specific response counters at zero. The indicator e has either the value 1 or the value 0, depending on whether the min-condition is fulfilled or not; it is fulfilled if sufficiently many steps have been entered.

Unlike the *response* counters, the counters s and t refer to the individual *steps* which make up a response (a response path). s is the number of any entered step. This number is automatically assigned by the computer and appears in brackets at the beginning of each calculation line (see Example 20 on page 124). The counter t (t: true) indicates the correct steps *entered*: s equals t if the calculation step [s] is a T-step. (Be careful not to confuse the value of t with the number of the T-step in the model answer.) The assignment $s \Leftarrow t+1$ has to do with the rule that individual answer steps are counted consecutively only *within one and the same answer*. The first calculation step of a new answer (a new attempt to answer) is always given the number [t+1]: the numbers of the answer steps of the new response follow the number [t] of the last *instructionally correct* step in the previous response.

It is first tested whether the entered response step S_s (step S with the step number s)[1] is syntactically correct, according to § 15 Point 1 on page 123, and if not, it is commented on accordingly. (Syntactical mistakes are *not* counted.) If the entered step is syntactically correct, the program asks whether S_s is the last step of this answer. This is the case if either a) the learner declares his response to be finished with the end-of-response sign, or if b) the computer judges that the step is numerically wrong. In the latter case the response end is *forced*. The learner is thus saved from further pointless and frustrating calculations which are unavoidable in conventional instruction. If S_s is *deliberately* entered by the learner as the *last* step of a response, it is checked whether the learner has entered enough steps to reach the prescribed minimum **min**: with the decision e=0 the computer judges whether the minimum condition has been fulfilled in one of the previous responses. This is not the case as long as e=0. This equation indicates that all responses given so far have been too short. If e=0, it is now necessary to check whether the response is long enough this time: whether s is greater than or equal to the minimum. If the minimum condition is not (yet) fulfilled, and if S_s is *not* numerically wrong, then one of the two min-comments is given out, depending on the result of

---

[1] An answer step is then and only then an S_s-step if it contains the end-of-step sign.

Flowchart of Calculation Path Tracing (a)

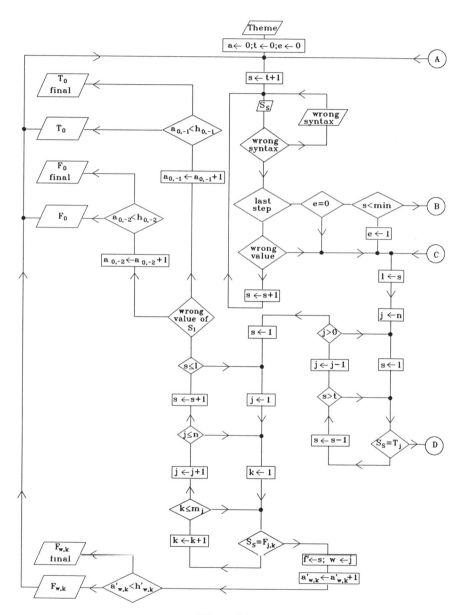

Figure 24a

Flowchart of Calculation Path Tracing (b)

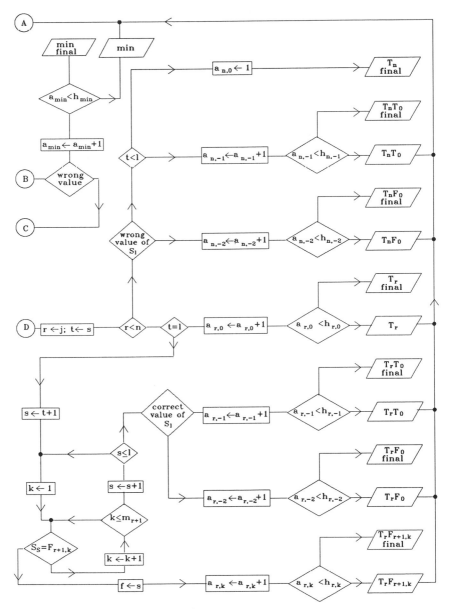

Figure 24b

the next decision (see the last paragraph of § 18 Point 1 on page 139). If the minimum condition is fulfilled, e is set at 1.

If S_s is numerically correct and a non-last step,

$$[s+1] \quad =$$

at the beginning of the next calculation line asks the learner to enter a further learning step. The s-loop — including the "syntax" loop — is run through again and again until *a response* (in the sense of calculation path tracing) has been "constructed".

Now the search for a T-step begins. Since we will later need the number of the last response step, we will make a note of it by $l \Leftarrow s$: the value of s at the deliberate or enforced end of the learning path is stored in the variable l (last number). In the double loop following this value assignment, the value of the above-mentioned counter t and the number r of the T-step within the model calculation are determined by the decision $S_s = T_j$ (providing, naturally, that a T-step exists); t tells us which of the *entered* (and checked) steps is correct, and r tells us which *model* step it corresponds to. The search in the double loop is regressive in two ways. We first compare the *last* calculation step S_l with the *last* model answer step T_n. This test ends at the very latest with the comparison of the first calculation step entered *in the respective response* to the T-step following the one found in the previous response.

If $r=n$, i.e. $S_t = T_n$, we only have to find out whether and how the learner went on calculating after entering T_n. There are three possibilities: (i) the last step is numerically wrong: the learner is given a $T_n F_0$-comment; (ii) the last step is numerically correct (and $l>t$): the learner is given a $T_n T_0$-comment; or iii) the last step entered is equal to the T_n-term ($l=t$). Note that in (i) it can only be the last step which is numerically wrong, since the calculation is stopped at once when a numerically incorrect step is entered. (This is not a destructive rejection of the learner's answer, as the (backward) search for correct components begins at once.)

If $r<n$ and $t=l$, the learner is given a T_r-feedback. Again, there is no search for anticipated mistakes: the last calculation term is a T-term. An interesting situation may occur if $r<n$ *and* $t<l$. The central point of backward calculation path tracing is the following:

> If a non-last T_r-term is found, there is consequently no later T-term. We presume therefore that an F_{r+1}-mistake has been made. This mistake is supposed to be the reason why the T_{r+1}-term (and possible "later" terms) is (are) missing.

The nicest confirmation of the instrugrammer's theory would naturally be to find an F_{r+1}-mistake in the entered step S_{t+1} which *immediately* follows $S_t = T_r$.

Hence, we *begin* by checking that with the help of the value assignment $s \Leftarrow t + 1$. The general decision reads: $S_s = F_{r+1, k}$. In the double loop belonging to this decision all entered answer steps following step t are checked on whether they are one of the m_{r+1} $F_{r+1, k}$-mistakes. If this is the case, we have got a very good, though not ideal, confirmation of the corresponding instruction theory. (The value of s found now, is stored in the variable f (f: false); we will need it for the standard comment (21) on page 140.) The corresponding comments are called T_r F_{r+1}-comments. If no F_{r+1}-mistake is found, we test whether the calculation steps following the T_r-step are numerically correct or not. The corresponding comments are: $T_r T_0$ and $T_r F_0$.

If the learner's calculation does not include any T-steps, the W-answers $F_{1, k}$ are examined in the decision $S_s = F_{j, k}$. These are — according to the instrugrammer — the mistakes made *immediately* (in Example 21 the wrong conversion of a mixed number into fraction).

The answer attributes

$$W_{j,k} = F_{j,k} \qquad j > 1$$

may be missing in the instrugram. This depends on whether or not the instrugrammer considered it useful to test such *isolated* mistakes that are related neither to the problem itself, nor to one of the model steps. In any case, the learner should be told at the end of the dialogue whether he has calculated numerically right or numerically wrong (T_0- and F_0-comment).

2. Response as a Sequence of Response Steps

The example of calculation path tracing shows that it is useful to consider *compound* responses. If a learner enters his solution of a problem in such a way that the individual steps of his procedure can be identified, his response can be analyzed much better, and he can be given better assistance. Diagnosis and therapy of mistakes are improved considerably .

In the light of instructional logic, the difference between a response and a response step consists in that a response is commented upon, while a response step is not (unless it is a response in itself). A response, as defined by calculation path tracing, exists if either the learner has indicated this by entering the end-of-response sign, or else it is noticed that the entered step is syntactically or numerically wrong. Both can already occur after the first step. Thus, a response may consist of only one step (e.g., only one T_r-step in Example 21). We can now *extend* the notion of response without contradicting the terminology used so far:

A response is a sequence of response steps.

We differentiate between *response step*, *response*, and *response sequence* (a sequence of step sequences), bearing in mind that a sequence may contain only one element.

The fact that only one-element and two-element *judging* sequences play a role in calculation path tracing has no general significance. If a response consists of n steps, 2^n step sequences can be differentiated. The development of interesting instructional types involving multi-step judging sequences containing more than two steps is surely the task of a science of instruction deserving such a name.

§ 18 Standardization[1] and Hybrid Representation

1. Comments on Inadmissible Answers

The standard *syntactical* comments of calculation path tracing are completely determined by the instructional type **Backward Calculation Path Tracing.** These comments all begin with:

(1)   The form of the answer is not correct.

Depending on the specific mistake, this is followed by (see § 15 Point 1 on page 124):

(2)   The terms in the calculation may only contain digits, commas, fraction bars and the four calculation signs: the plus, minus, multiplication and division signs.

(3)   You must not enter an equals sign.

(4)   Two calculation signs must not appear consecutively.

(5)   The calculation term must not begin with either a division or a multiplication sign.

(6)   The calculation term must not end with a calculation sign.

(7)   Two fractions must not appear consecutively. There has to be a calculation sign between them.

(8)   Neither a divisor nor a denominator may have the value zero.

If there are several (types of) mistakes, the one that occurs first is commented upon.

---

[1] A standard comment is both interim and final comment, unless otherwise specified.

The standard comments belonging to a miniresponse are also determined by the instructional type. The **min**-standard interim comment is:

(9)   The calculation will only then be analyzed, if (at least) one answer has been entered with at least **min** calculation steps.

The **min**-model comment is:

(10)   Since this is the h_{min}-th response, which does not contain the required minimum number of **min** calculation steps, you will now get the model calculation:
        Model answer.

2. Comments on Admissible Answers

a) R-*Standard Comments* (*Model Comments and* St-*Comments*)

The R1-model comment is:

(11)   Well done! You have found the required solution. This is the model calculation:
        Model answer. .

The R1-**St**-comment consists of the first two sentences of (11):

(11a)   Well done! You have found the required solution.

The R2-**St**-interim comment $R2 = T_n T_0$ begins with (11a). It reads:

(12)   Well done! You have found the required solution. But you went on calculating after finding it. Please enter only the solution step again.

The R2-**St**-final comment consists of the first three sentences of (12). The R2-model comment is:

(13)   Well done! You gave the correct solution in calculation step [t]. But you went on calculating. Please compare your calculation with the model calculation:
        Model answer.

The R3-**St**-interim comment $R3 = T_n F_0$ begins with (11a). It runs:

(14)   Well done! You have found the required solution. But you went on calculating and made a mistake in the last step of your calculation. Please enter the solution as the last calculation step.

The R3-St-final comment is like the interim comment, however, without the last sentence. The R3-model comment is:

(15)   Well done! You entered the required solution in step [t] of your calculation. But you went on calculating and made a mistake in the last step. Compare your calculation with the model calculation:
Model answer.

b) P-*Comments*

The T_r-St-interim comment $(0 < r < n)$ is:

(16)   In step [t] of your calculation you entered a correct interim result. The last calculation step is numerically correct, but it is not the required solution. Try again, starting with step [t+1].

The T_r-St-final comment is the same as (16), but *without* the last sentence. The T_r-model comment $(0 < r < n)$ is:

(17)   In step [t] of your calculation you entered a correct interim result. The last step of your calculation is numerically correct, but it is not the required solution. Compare your calculation with the model calculation:
Model answer.

The $T_r T_0$-St-interim comment is:

(18)   Step [t] of your calculation is correct. But you have not got the right solution. Try again, starting with step [t+1].

The $T_r T_0$-model comment is:

(19)   Step [t] of your calculation is correct. However, you have not found the required solution. This is the model calculation:
Model answer.

The $T_r T_0$-St-final comment consists of the first two sentences of (18). The corresponding $T_r F_0$-final comments are the same as (18), except that the second sentence is replaced by :

(20)   The last step of your calculation is incorrect.

The general $T_r F_{r+1,k}$-St-interim comments with $0 < t < n$ and $k > 0$ are:

(21)   Step [t] of your calculation is correct. But in step [f] you made a mistake. Try again, starting with step [t+1].

The first two sentences of (21) make up the corresponding **St**-final comment. The $T_r F_{r+1,k}$-model comment is:

(22)   Step **[t]** of your calculation is correct. But in step **[f]** you made a mistake. This is the model calculation: **Model answer.**

If (21) is to be combined with a *specific* (individual) comment so that the latter appears between the second and the last sentence of (21), this is recorded in the dialogue as follows:

(22a)   **St.** ...

The three dots represent the specific comment.

c) $W_{j,k}$-*Comments*

The **St**-interim comment is:

(23)   Step **[f']** of your calculation is incorrect. Try to solve the problem again. Start from the beginning.

This comment may also be combined with specific comment elements (see (22a)). The **St**-final comment equals the first sentence of (23). The model comment is made up of the **St**-final comment and of "This is the model calculation: **model answer.**"

d) U-*Comments*

The **UT**-standard feedback (to T_0-answers) is:

(24)   Your answer is numerically correct. However, I cannot properly evaluate your answer, since I did not foresee any of the steps you took.

The model comment consists of (24) and of "This is the model calculation: **model answer.**" The **UF**-standard comment (to F_0-answers) is:

(25)   Unfortunately I cannot evaluate your answer, since I did not foresee any of your learning steps. But your last step is numerically incorrect.

The model comment consists of (25) and of "This is the model calculation: **model answer.**"

e) StT- *and* StF-*Comments*

In the dialogue the two standard comments

(26)   Step **[t]** of your calculation is correct.

and

(27)   Step **[f']** of your calculation is incorrect.

are noted as **StT** and **StF**. (StT and StF may of course be missing if (26) and/or (27) is part of one of the comments given under b) or c).)

3. Standard Versions of Backward Calculation Path Tracing

We differentiate between two standard versions of the instructional type Backward Calculation Path Tracing. Since the dialogue is completely prede-fined in both versions, only the head and theme and, in the auxiliary area, the model calculation (and in the *fine standard* also the error survey) are noted down.

a) *Rough Standard*: **Backward Calculation Path Tracing, Rough Standard**

The rough standard is based on the following sequence of attributes:

$$
(28)
\quad
\begin{array}{ccc}
T_n, & T_n T_0, & T_n F_0, \\
T_{n-1}, & T_{n-1} T_0, & T_{n-1} F_0, \\
\vdots & \vdots & \\
T_1, & T_1 T_0, & T_1 F_0, \\
& T_0, & F_0.
\end{array}
$$

(T_1, T_2, T_3, ...,T_n are the *relevant* model steps.) The rough standard is used when the author provides only the model calculation, and not an error survey. The sequence (28) and the I-attributes (syntax and minimum attributes), which are common to all versions of calculation path tracing (and which are explained in § 15 Point 1), determine the basis of the rough standard. The interim and model comments corresponding to (28) are given under Point 2a and 2b. As for the high numbers, the regulations $h_{R1} = 1$ and $h_{R2} = 2$ have *general* validity (i.e. they cannot be changed); if no special arrangements are made for the other attributes, then $h_{A'} = 3$, provided $A' \neq$ R1, R2, I. If something else shall apply, the specific high numbers have to be given in the head.

b) *Fine Standard*: **Backward Calculation Path Tracing, Fine Standard**
The full standard version is based on the (generally valid) I-attribute
sequence and on the sequence:

(29)

$$T_n, \; T_n T_0, \; T_n F_0,$$
$$T_{n-1}F_{n;1}, \; ..., \; T_{n-1}F_{n;m_n}, T_{n-1}, T_{n-1}T_0, T_{n-1}F_0,$$
$$\vdots$$
$$T_1 F_{2;1}, \; ..., \; T_1 F_{2;m_2}, \; T_1, \; T_1 T_0, \; T_1 F_0,$$
$$F_{1;1}, \; ..., \; F_{1;m_1}, \qquad T_0, \quad F_0$$

The $T_r F_{r+1;k}$-interim comment in the fine standard differs from (21):

(30)

> Step **[t]** of your calculation is correct. In step **[f]**, however,
> you made a mistake:
> $$F_{r+1;k}\text{-error}$$
> Try again, starting with step **[t+1]**.

In the comment given to the learner, the comment variable $F_{r+1;k}$**-error** is
replaced by its "value", i.e. by the corresponding term from the error survey.
For example, if $t=2$ and $k=1$, the term

$$\frac{* \cdot 2}{1 \cdot *}$$

is given out instead of $F_{r+1;k}$**-error** (see Example 21, pages 126 ff.): the
learner is given some, although not all, information about the mistake he
made in the places marked by *asterisks*. (Note that the fine standard in calculation path tracing does not include $W_{j;k}$-attributes with $j>1$.) The $W_{1;k}$-
interim comment of the fine standard is:

(31)

> In step **[f']** of your calculation you made the following
> mistake:
> $$F_{1;k}\text{-error}$$
> Start calculating from the beginning.

The $T_r F_{r+1;k}$- and $F_{1,k}$-St-final comments, always encoded by **St** and therefore
only appearing in *mixed* dialogues, are the same as the comments (30) and
(31), however, without the corresponding last sentence.

The model comments corresponding to the comments (30) and (31) and all
other I-comments possible in the fine standard are the same as those given in
Points 1 and 2.

4. Hybrid Representation

The example given below is closely related to Example 21.[1] However, the notation of the answer attributes has been changed in such a way that it has become superfluous to note down the encoded key kernels explicitly.

Hybrid Fine Standard

078.　*Dividing Mixed Numbers.*
　　　Backward Calculation Path Tracing, Hybrid Fine Standard;
　　　min$=3$; h$_{min}=3$.

Show what you have learned by solving the following problem.

$$4\frac{1}{2} : 3\frac{3}{4}$$

Enter the complete calculation.

Model Answer:　　　　　　　　　**E r r o r S u r v e y**

$4\frac{1}{2} : 3\frac{3}{4}$	1	2	3
T1 $= \frac{9}{2} : \frac{15}{4}$	$\frac{*}{2} : \frac{*}{4}$	$\frac{*}{2} : (3\frac{3}{4} \text{ v } \frac{15}{4})$	$(4\frac{1}{2} \text{ v } \frac{9}{2}) : \frac{*}{4}$
T2 $= \frac{9}{2} \cdot \frac{4}{15}$	$\frac{2}{9} \cdot \frac{4}{15}$	$\frac{2}{9} \cdot \frac{15}{4}$	$\frac{135}{8} \text{ v } 16\frac{7}{8}$
$= \frac{9 \cdot 4}{2 \cdot 15}$			
T3 $= \frac{3 \cdot 2}{1 \cdot 5}$	$\frac{* \cdot 2}{1 \cdot *}$	$\frac{3 \cdot *}{* \cdot 5}$	$\frac{36}{30}$
T4 $= \frac{6}{5}$	$\frac{*}{5}$	$\frac{6}{*}$	
T5 $= 1\frac{1}{5}$	$*\frac{1}{5}$	$\frac{1}{5}$	

---

[1] See pages 126 to 130.

P(2,3),2

> You have forgotten to reduce the fraction [t] to its lowest terms. Remember: always reduce fractions to their lowest terms before multiplying.

P(1,1),2

> You have changed the two mixed numbers to improper fractions correctly. But you seem to have forgotten how to divide by a fraction. Only the fraction by which you are dividing has to be inverted. But you inverted both fractions!

P(1,2)2

> StT. But you inverted the dividend (the fraction *in front* of the division sign) instead of the divisor (the fraction after the division sign). To divide by a fraction, multiply by the reciprocal of the fraction. The first fraction remains unchanged.

P(1,3),2

> StT. You just multiplied the fractions. But you are supposed to divide by $\frac{15}{4}$.

Example 22

For example, the answer attribute noted down in Example 21 under P13 is now called: P(2,3). The digit '2' indicates the step T_2 and the corresponding mistake

$$F_{2+1;3} = F_{3;3}.$$

Consequently:

$$P(2,3) = T_2 F_{3;3},$$
$$P(1,1) = T_1 F_{2;1},$$
$$P(1,2) = T_1 F_{2;2},$$
$$P(1,3) = T_1 F_{2;3}.$$

The three R-attributes can now be written as:

$$R1 = R(n,0); \quad R2 = R(n,-1); \quad R3 = R(n,-2),$$

with n to be replaced by the respective value. The T_0- and F_0-answers are now noted down as U(0,-1) and U(0,-2), the $T_r T_0$- and $T_r F_0$-answers as P(r,-1) and P(r,-2). Finally, the *isolated* $F_{1;k}$-answers will be called $F_{1;k} = W(0,k)$. The values of the high numbers are determined as described in Point 3a.

As for the feedback in Example 22, the test for I (inadmissibility) is followed by further analysis according to sequence (29). It is first checked whether the answer is an R1-answer, i.e. an R(5,0)-answer. If this is the case, then the program checks whether the R1-attribute appears in the *explicitly* recorded dialogue. If so, the learner is given the comment noted down especially for this purpose. If not — as in our example — the R1-model comment belonging to the fine standard is given out. If there is no R1-answer, then the procedure goes on accordingly. For example, if the learner's answer is a P(2,3)-answer, the system does *not* react by giving out the *standard* interim comment, but by giving out as the interim comment the *explicitly* recorded P(2,3)-comment.

APPENDIX

Instrugram Examples
and
Description of Presentation

A   Hydrostatic Pressure

B   Hierarchy with Program Call-Up

C   Learner Control

The instrugram A is strictly tutorial. The examples B and C show that Instruction Language also provides the interfaces between tutorial and non-tutorial instruction. It is possible to both incorporate programs into an instrugram and to describe learner control, which is not subject to the tutorial logic, by means of the N-attribute.

A. Hydrostatic Pressure[1]

1. *Introduction to the Subject Area*

Commonly, the study of hydrostatics starts by looking at examples from everyday experience that illustrate how easily liquid particles can be pushed aside. By analysing piston pressure one finally arrives at the definition of pressure.

Furthermore it is to be demonstrated that liquids, on account of their weight, generate a pressure within their own volume. This pressure is called hydrostatic pressure, or weight pressure, and is the subject of this instrugram.

Finally the textbooks discuss common physical phenomena and applications: the hydrostatic paradox, communicating vessels, Boyle's law, buoyancy and floating, and Archimedes' principle.

2. *Prerequisite Knowledge*

a) *Quantities and Units of Measurement*

force	F	N
mass	m	kg
volume	V	dm^3
weight	W	N
acceleration due to gravity	$g = W/m$	N/kg
density	$\rho = m/V$	g/cm^3 = kg/dm^3

b) *From Hydrostatics*

— Particles in liquids and gases can be pushed aside easily in any direction;
— A liquid can be put in a state of pressure by the exertion of piston force;
— If liquids are in a state of pressure, force is exerted on any boundary area; (Note the difference between pressure and force!)
— Definition of pressure: If force F acts on area A of a liquid, the quotient F/A is called the pressure p,

$$p = F/A \qquad \text{Unit: } 1\,\text{N/m}^2 = 1\,\text{Pa (Pascal)}$$

— If there is pressure p in a liquid, area A, regardless of its position, is exposed to force F proportional to A, with $F = p \cdot A$. This force is perpendicular to the area.

---

[1] Adapted from a seminar paper by A. Gruppe (summer term 1981).

3. *Specific Learning Goals*

a) The student should find the following properties of hydrostatic pressure by means of an experiment:

— Pressure increases in proportion to the diving depth;

— Pressure is constant at any level parallel to the surface of the liquid;

— Pressure is independent from the shape of the vessel (this finding shall serve as a preparation to the hydrostatic paradox);

— Isotropy of hydrostatic pressure (which may exert an "upward-driving" force on the body — this is important to the explanation of buoyancy).

b) The formula for hydrostatic pressure shall be found by the student.

c) The independence of pressure from the volume of the liquid column is to be found by means of the formula. It is only the height of the liquid column that matters (which is important to the hydrostatic paradox).

d) The student should practice the formula for hydrostatic pressure by solving simple problems.

4. *Contents of the Instrugram*[1]

---

[1] The table of contents is made up of the sequence *headings.*

5. *Experimental Apparatus*

The following apparatus has to be prepared for the student's experiment:

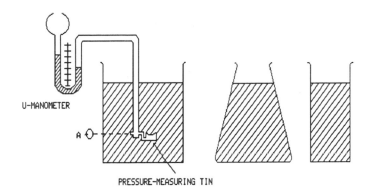

A pressure-measuring tin, whose opening has been covered with a rubber membrane, is connected, turnable around the axis A, to a U-manometer containing colored water. If pressure is exerted on the rubber membrane, air is displaced from the measuring tin, causing the water column in the U-manometer to move in proportion to the pressure.

In addition, the experiment requires three vessels of the indicated shape, at least 23 cm high, a plastic ruler and a bottle of spirit.

6. *Instrugram*

001.   Everyday Experience: *Diving into a Swimming Pool.*
       Single Selection; A..D.

While diving into a swimming pool, you have perhaps felt an unpleasant pressure on your ears. Can you tell us more about it?

A. I've never dived in my life.

B. That's only an illusion. Since water in a swimming pool is not compressed by a piston, there can be no pressure in water.

C. The deeper you go into the water, the stronger and more unpleasant the pressure gets.

D. The pressure depends on the size of the swimming pool. It is much less in a small swimming pool than in a big lake, which contains a lot more water.

R1,1 = 'C'
   St.
W1,2 = 'A'
   C1 Have you really never dived or are you just making the
       answering easier? Think again.
   C2 That's alright. We will have a closer look at the pressure
       conditions that occur in diving right away.
W2,2
   C1 St. Have you really experienced this or have you been misled
       by the suggested argument?
   C2 St. We will have a closer look at the pressure conditions that
       occur in diving right away.

002.   Objectifying Everyday Experience: Analogy of *Ear and
       Pressure-Measuring Tin.*

      Single Selection, Rough Standard; B:A..C; S:B.

In order to investigate the pressure under water, we will use,
instead of our ears, a pressure-measuring tin with an *artificial*
eardrum to examine the pressure in a glass vessel filled with water.
Check the following statements by experimentation!

If the immersion depth is the same, the pressure on the measuring
tin

A. is greater in a large vessel than in a small vessel.

B. is the same in each vessel.

C. is less in a vessel that becomes narrower towards the top than in
   a cylindric vessel.

003.   *Experiment: How Pressure is Affected by Moving the Measuring
       Tin Horizontally.*

      Single Selection, Rough Standard; B:A..C; S:C.

How is pressure affected when the measuring tin is moved
horizontally at the same immersion depth?

A. The pressure is greater in the middle than towards the side of
   the vessel.

B. The pressure is less in the middle than towards the side of the
   vessel.

C. The pressure is the same when the measuring tin is moved
   horizontally.

004.   *Experiment to Determine the Dependence of Water Pressure on Immersion Depth.*

Injective Matching; Locus Answer.

How does the pressure change when the measuring tin is immersed increasingly deeper?   03

Determine the pressure for 2 cm, 4 cm, 6 cm, 8 cm, 10 cm, 15 cm and 20 cm depth and indicate the corresponding interval.

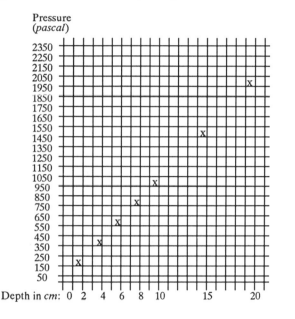

Pressure *(pascal)*   09

Depth in *cm:*   18

R1,1 =   s = 7
St. Well done! You have experimented very carefully!

P1,3: s > 0
Color (S-element) →   yellow.
The yellow crosses indicate the correct answers and the white ones the incorrect answers.

W1,4
  C1 St. Are you sure that you have adjusted the depth correctly? Remember that the distance between the membrane of the measuring tin and the water surface is important! Or perhaps you are reading the pressure from the wrong arm of the U-manometer?
  C2 St. Check your measuring apparatus: does the U-manometer really read 0 Pa pressure when the tin has not been immersed? Check by shaking whether water has entered the measuring tin.
  C3 Still not correct! Ask the technical assistant for help and do the experiment again!

005.   *Evaluating the Experiment: Pressure as a Function of Depth.*
        Single Selection, Rough Standard; B:A..D; S:C.

Having carried out these systematic measurements, you will be able
to tell the functional relationship between the immersion depth h
and the pressure p (k is a constant).

   A. $p = k \cdot h^2$

   B. $p = k \cdot h/p$

   C. $p = k \cdot h$

   D. $p = k \cdot 1/h$

006.   Stability of the Experiment (Isotropy of Pressure): *How is
        Pressure Affected by Turning the Measuring Tin?*
        Common Selection; 1A..1E, 2A..2C.

Until now, the membrane of the measuring tin has always pointed
upwards. What happens if the tin is turned around its horizontal
axis first sideward and then with the membrane pointing
downwards? (The immersion depth stays the same.)

1. Membrane points to the side:

   A. Pressure increases.

   B. Pressure decreases.

   C. Pressure stays the same.

   D. Membrane becomes most distorted in the middle.

   E. The distortion of the membrane is asymmetrical and larger at
      its lower part.

2. Membrane points downwards:

   A. Pressure increases.

   B. Pressure decreases.

   C. Pressure stays the same.

Model answer: 1C, 1D, 2C.

R1,1 = s = 3
    St.

W1,4 = s = 0
    C1 St.
    C2 St. Check your measuring equipment: does the U-manometer really read 0 Pa pressure when the tin has not been immersed? Or is the membrane perhaps not watertight? Check by shaking whether water has entered the measuring tin.
    C3 Still not correct! Ask the technical assistant for help and carry out the experiment again!

P1,3

    St. The **result/results** of the **measurement/measurements** **S̲-element is/are** wrong.

007. *The Experimental Results.*
    Free Selection; A..E.

This is what we can learn from the experiment:
The force on the membrane

A. acts only from top to bottom.

B. acts mainly from top to bottom.

C. acts always perpendicular to the membrane, no matter what direction this points to.

D. is greatest when the membrane points upwards.

E. is always the same no matter what direction the membrane points to.

R1,1 = 'C' & 'E'

P1,2 = ('A' v 'B') & 'E'
    St. We saw in the experiment that the membrane, when pointing sideways, was most distorted in the middle part. What does this tell us about the direction of the force?

P2,2 = 'C' & 'D'
    St. We saw in the experiment that pressure at a given depth is independent from where the membrane points to. What can you now say about the size of the force?

W1,2 = ('A' v 'B') & 'C' v 'D' & 'E'
    Your answers are contradictory!

W2,3
    C1 St.
    C2 St. Observe again carefully what happens if the measuring tin is turned around!
    Hierarchy 5/6.

008.   *Formula for Pressure.*

Single Selection; A..E.

Let us now think about how the pressure at the depth h below the
water level comes about. So far, we have always generated the
pressure by exerting a force on a piston, but where is the piston?
Let us take a closer look at the glass vessel:
<key>

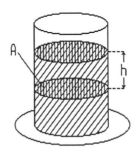

03

09

We can imagine the liquid column above the area A at the depth h
to be a piston with the mass

$$m = \rho \cdot V = \rho \cdot A \cdot h.$$

The piston presses with its weight $W = m \cdot g = \rho \cdot A \cdot h \cdot g$ on   16
the area A, thereby generating the pressure:

A. $p = W/A$ D. $p = \rho \cdot h \cdot g$

B. $p = A/W$ E. $p = F/A$

C. $p = (\rho \cdot A \cdot h \cdot g)/A$ 20

R1,1= 'D'
    St.
P1,2= 'A'
    St. You have to replace W by the term for the weight of the
    liquid-column piston.
P2,2= 'C'
    St. Something may be cancelled in this fraction!
P3,2= 'E'
    St. This is the general formula for pressure which is exerted
    by the force F on the area A. In our case it is the weight W of
    the liquid column that exerts pressure. We have to set
    $F = W$.
W1,2
    St. Pressure is always force divided by area.

009.   *Applying the Pressure Formula.*

It would now be interesting to check whether we can really use our new formula $p = \rho \cdot h \cdot g$ to describe the pressure conditions in water which we observed in our experiment.

You will remember that we measured a pressure of around 1000 Pa at 10 cm depth. Find the exact pressure, using the formula!

R1,1: '981 Pa'

W1,4

    C1 St. To recall: $\rho_{water} = 1 \text{ kg/dm}^3 = 1000 \text{ kg/m}^3$,

        $g = 9.81 \text{ N/kg}$, $1 \text{ Pa} = 1 \text{ N/m}^2$

    C2 St. Are you paying attention to the units? The easiest way is to change cm to dm right from the start!

    C3 St. Let's try it together!

        $p = \rho_{water} \cdot h \cdot g = 1 \text{ kg/dm}^3 \cdot 1 \text{ dm} \cdot 9.81 \text{ N/kg}$

    C4 That is still not right! We had:

        $p = 1 \text{ kg/dm}^3 \cdot 1 \text{ dm} \cdot 9.81 \text{ N/kg}$.

        That makes:

        $p = 9.81 \text{ N/dm}^2 = 981 \text{ N/m}^2 = 981 \text{ Pa}$.

010.   Qualitative Transfer: *Pressure in Different Liquids.*

    Unequivocal Matching; A1..B3.

We were quite lucky.

We regarded the water column above area A as a large piston whose weight acts on area A. This served as a fine model for how water pressure, which we had observed in the initial experiment, occurs. As the measured pressure corresponds to the one we calculated with the formula derived from our model, we could be well content. But let's not get lazy — let's take a closer look at our model. If it really is the weight of the water column that exerts the pressure, then the pressure at the same immersion depth in a

                            1. is greater than in water.

A. heavier liquid

                            2. is less than in water.

B. lighter liquid

                            3. is the same as in water.

Match the letters A and B with the correct identification numbers.

R1,1= 'A1' & 'B2'
　　St. We will check our assumption at once by means of a
　　calculation and afterwards an experiment!

P1,2: 'A1' v 'B2'
　　St. <u>S</u>-element is wrong.

W1,2
　　St.

011.　　Quantitative Transfer: *Pressure in Spirit*.

Spirit is lighter than water. It has a density of
ρ_{sp} = 0.79 kg/dm^3. Find the pressure of spirit at a depth of
10 cm.

R1,1= '775 Pa'
　　St.

W1,3
　　C1 St. To recall: g = 9.81 N/kg, 1 Pa = 1 N/m^2.
　　C2 St. Let us try it together!

$$p = \rho_{Sp} \cdot h \cdot g$$
$$= 0.79 \frac{kg}{dm^3} \cdot 1 \text{ dm} \cdot 9.81 \frac{N}{kg}$$

　　Now you do the multiplication!

012.　　*Verifying the Theory*.

　　Free Selection; A..D.

Check the result by experimenting with the measuring tin.
What pressure do you measure at a depth of 10 cm in spirit?

　　A. The pressure is between 770 and 780 Pa.
　　B. The pressure is less than 770 Pa.
　　C. The measured pressure is precisely 775.0 Pa.
　　D. The pressure is greater than 780 Pa.

R1,1= 'A'
　　St.

R2,2= 'C' v 'A' & 'C'
　　C1 St. Were you really able to read the pressure so precisely? Or
　　did you simply take the result from the last question? In this
　　case you should repeat the measurement and read the
　　manometer again!
　　C2 St.

W1,3 = 'B' v 'D'.
    C1 What shall we do now? We were sure that we calculated the previous problem correctly. So has our model been wrong? Being good experimental physicists, however, we know that a lot of mistakes may slip into an experiment that distort the result. So before concluding that our theory is wrong, we should make sure that we have measured correctly! Check the experiment for possible causes of mistakes (membrane not watertight, U-manometer reads incorrect figures) and repeat the experiment!
    C2 St. Ask the technical assistant for help.
W2,2
    St. Your answers are contradictory!

013.   Practice by Application: *Pressure in the Sea and in a Salt-Water Shaft*

    Double Common Selection; 1A..1D, 2A..2C.

With the correspondence of precalculated and experimentally confirmed pressure in spirit we proved that it is really the weight of the liquid that is responsible for the so-called hydrostatic pressure. For this reason, hydrostatic pressure is sometimes also named weight pressure. As seen in the experiment, it is independent of the shape of the vessel or the position of the area that it acts upon. We can see from the formula $p = \rho \cdot h \cdot g$ that hydrostatic pressure depends solely on the depth h, the density ρ of the liquid and the acceleration due to gravity g. We can therefore now calculate the pressure in the sea (density of salt water: $\rho = 1.02 \text{ g/cm}^3$):

1. The pressure at a depth of 10 m in the Pacific Ocean is:

    A. 100 Pa;   B. 98100 Pa;   C. 100 kPa;   D. 981 kPa

2. By comparison, the pressure at a depth of 10 m in a narrow shaft filled likewise with salt water is:

    A. greater;   B. the same;   C. less.

Model answer: 1C, 2B

R1,1 = s=2
P1,2:   s=1
    Your answer to part **S-first element** of the question is correct.
W1,2
    St.

7. *Presentation*

Presentation of instruction means the way the instruction is carried out spatio-temporally. How do input and output take place? We distinguish between *standard* or *default* and *special* presentation. Minimum instruction is given in standard presentation if the module (or the one-module hierarchy) in question contains *no* instructions concerning the presentation (default presentation), which is the case in the entire example *Hydrostatic Pressure* except for Hierarchies 004 and 008. Let us first discuss the (modular)

a) *Default Presentation*

The usual way of entering an answer is via the input keyboard, with the answer appearing on the screen below the theme. The answer's end is indicated by the entering of the FINISHED-sign (by pressing the RETURN-key). Any *non-first* answer (within minimum instruction) is carried out by *adding to or changing* the old answer: a new answer is usually a *revision* of the old one. If the new answer *equals* the old one, the learner only needs to enter the FINISHED-sign. If he wishes to reject the answer, he has to delete the old answer (unless he rejected that, too).

   The standard output of theme and comments on the screen is *consistent in form:* the form of the presentation image equals that of the representation image. Theme and plain-text comments are presented the way they are noted down in the module. In particular, output image and representation image correspond in the following: equal number of lines, equal number of characters in line, equal number of space lines, equal start-of-line position. As for the default presentation on the screen, there has to be space for the presentation of the full theme, the full corresponding answer and at least part of the comment belonging to this answer *simultaneously*. The entire screen area is divided into three rectangular sections: theme section, answer section and comment section.

Screen Division

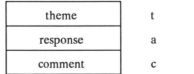

Figure 25

The width is the same for each section (corresponding to the screen width available for writing) and totals 80 characters. Texts that are wider than 80 characters cannot be presented by default presentation; special output instructions are needed in this case. As the common *instrugraphical* representation on paper comprises at most 75 characters per line, the screen width is usually sufficient for the standard output.

The *height* of t and a in Figure 25 depends on the number of written[1] lines of the theme or of the respective answer. Since the standard screen has 25 lines, with 2 lines serving to separate the sections and the last one being reserved for special purposes, a maximum of

$$c_{max} = 25 - (t+a+3)$$

lines is left for the presentation of the comment. If theme and answer require too much space, the comment belonging to the answer can only *successively* be presented. The learner puts it on to the screen bit by bit (by pressing a key).

Let us summarize the procedure of default presentation:

a) Theme output in the upper section of the screen (Figure 25).

b) Answer input and presentation in the answer section. The FINISHED-sign initiates:

c) The output of the interim comment in the comment section (simultaneously or successively by learner control).

d) Entering of the new answer, etc.

The default presentation of minimum instruction ends with the output of a final comment.

The transition to the next module is also initiated by the FINISHED-sign. As space is now required for the new theme, the comment as well as the answer and the old theme are erased.

b) *Description of Special Presentation Instructions*

CLEARING LINE[2]

Dividing a hierarchy horizontally, the *clearing line* marks the beginning of a new screen page and clears the old one, with the exception of the sequence heading (see Hierarchy 008 on page 158, Example 15 on page 104 and Appendix C on pages 171 ff.). The learner sets the time of clearing by *pressing a key*. This is indicated by the presentation of '<KEY>' in the lower part of

---

[1] Including the *represented space lines*.

[2] The clearing line has been suggested by R.-U. Glück.

the right screen margin. It is *re*presented in the instrugram by <key> on the left above the clearing line (see the above-mentioned examples). (Of course, the author may also set a time limit.)

In the case of the *return* to a source module, the lesson is continued with the part below the last clearing line (in the source module on page 171 of Appendix C, for example, starting with the presentation of the selection answers A, B, and C).

MARGINAL NUMBER

A marginal number on the right of an instrugram line indicates the position of the respective line on the screen (see the above-mentioned examples). The marginal number ensures that the instrugram image determining the screen image can be represented in a clearly readable and therefore informative manner.

LOCUS ANSWER

The instruction **locus answer** (e.g. in Hierarchy 004 on page 155) indicates that the learner's answer is to be identified by its place on the screen. Matching in Hierarchy 004 is not achieved by entering response indicators (as in the contentually related Example 17 on pages 116 f.) but by positioning the cursor at certain places on the matching site. This procedure has several advantages: there is no need to specify the set of admissible response signs in the sequence head; there are no longer inadmissible response *indicators* as the cursor may only be positioned on *admissible* areas within the matching site. This makes entering answers technically easy and less susceptible to mistakes. The learner does not have to worry about the (complicated) structure of response indicators. The typological I-comments can be realized very easily (by contrast to Example 17), e.g. acoustically, perhaps by means of a warning signal. (The difference should be noted between *inadmissible answers* — which still exist[1] — and *inadmissible response indicators*, which do not occur in locus answers.)

The model answer is likewise not indicated verbally but by visual/graphical means, i.e. by all correct crosses on the matching site. (Of course, these are not shown to the learner *before* he answers.) Thus, the instrugram reader may easily identify the right answer.

---

[1] However, the instruction **locus answer** in Hierarchy 001 of Appendix C ensures also that no inadmissible answers may occur. The cursor may only be positioned at the response indicators 'A', 'B' or 'C'.

CHANGE OF COLOR

Another presentation instruction is contained in the P1-comment of Hierarchy 004 on page 155:

Color (S-element) → yellow.

This tells the computer that the *right* crosses (the S-crosses), which are initially (in the learner's answer) presented in white, are to be presented in yellow after the learner has confirmed his answer (by pressing <return>). The arrow stands for the *change* of color (from white to yellow).

B. Hierarchy with Program Call-Up: Shot-Putting.

1. *Preliminary Remark*

In our discussion of the relationship between the distance obtained in shot-putting and the angle of release, we assume, for reasons of simplicity, that release and landing take place at the same level. The simulation would, however, be more realistic if the height of release was about 2.20 m.[1]

2. *Description of the External Program*

After calling up the program[2] (indicated in the instrugram) the following screen is presented:

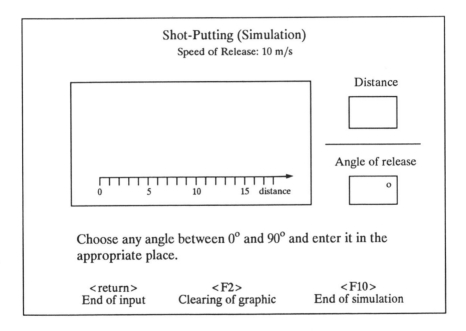

After the learner has entered the selected angle in the appropriate place (confirming it with <return>), the computer plots the pertaining trajectory

---

[1] See BALLREICH and KUHLOW (1986), pages 89 ff., especially Table 7.2, and HAY (1978), pages 38 ff., especially Table 1 on page 40 and Figure 22 on page 41. At a speed of release between 12 m/s and 14 m/s the optimum angle of release is between 41° and 42°.

[2] The expression '**program**' implies, among other things, that the program is called up (at the respective passage in the theme or the comment) by pressing any key.

(on the largest section of the screen). The distances at each moment are counted in the numerical output area (at the top on the right); the final figure indicates the distance reached. The progress of movement for any angle can be shown to the pupil on request. The curves usually remain on the screen but can be *completely* erased by pressing <F2>. With <F10> (tutorial) instruction continues.

3. *Hierarchy*

003.   Simulation of Shot. *Distance and Angle of Release.*

Single Selection; B: A..E, S: B.

We will now examine if and to what extent the distance of the shot put depends on the size of the angle between the direction of the shot and the horizontal.

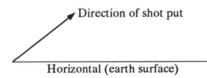

Direction of shot put

Horizontal (earth surface)

Program (shot put)

What have you learned from this experiment?

Choose the answer that corresponds most to your observations.

A. The distance of the shot depends on the angle of release. The greater the angle, the greater the distance.

B. The distance of the shot depends on the angle of release. The greatest distance is obtained at medium-sized angles.

C. The distance of the shot depends on the angle of release. The smaller the angle, the greater the distance.

D. The distance of the shot *does not* depend on the angle of release.

E. I cannot identify anything definite.

Addition: The maximum distance is obtained at an angle of 45°.

R1,1 = 'B'
> St.
> Sequence [1]

W1,3 = 'A' v 'C'

> C1 Have you examined a "representative" selection of angles?
> Repeat the experiment and fill in your angles with the
> corresponding distances on a table of values.
> **Program[1] (shot put)**

> C2 St. Choose 5°, 30°, 45°, 60°, 85° as angles and find out the
> corresponding distances.
> **Program (shot put)**

W2,2 = 'D'

> If the distance was independent of the angle, we would always
> obtain the same distance in spite of different angles (at the
> same initial speed). Check again!
> **Program (shot put)**

V1,2

> Repeat the experiment with the following angles:
> 5°, 25°, 45°, 60° and 80°. For purposes of control, please
> enter the angles and the obtained distances in a table of
> values.
> **Program (shot put)**

[1]   Working Towards More Precision. *The Optimum Angle.*

At which angle(s) is the maximum distance obtained?

Model answer: The maximum distance is obtained at an angle of
45°.

R1,1: 40 < **string of digits** < 50

W1,2: 0 < **string of digits** < 90
> St.

U1,2

> St. There is exactly one angle at which the maximum distance
> can be obtained.

---

[1] In order to ensure a proper continuation of instruction after the *end of the program,* a
program call-up in a comment (by contrast to the usual complete storage of the given screen
contents) causes the clearing of the comment part already outputted.

C. Learner Control

1. *Instrugram*[1]

001. *Entering a Selection Response.*
Single Selection; A..C; **Locus Answer** .

The keyboard is your most important entering device. It constitutes 03
the "interface" between you and the computer. To make it easier
for you to immediately and correctly recognize whether we are
talking about a KEY, the key is specially marked.
Instead of 07

key A, key B, key C, ...

we usually write

key <A>, key <B>, key <C>, ...

This also goes for the so-called *function* keys, such as

key <F1>, key <F2>, key <F3>, ...

Sometimes the word 'key' is left out, and we simply note down
<A>, <F2> etc.
If *any* key out of the keyboard is to be pressed, the ex- 15
pression <key> appears in the bottom right-hand corner of the
screen.

<key>

A. Entering an answer 03

B. The role of the function keys 05

C. End 07

You will now learn how to select from the three choices 09

A, B and C,

i.e. how to enter a selection response into the computer.
If you press an <arrow key>, the white *cursor* moves. You can
select an answer by 13

---

[1] This instrugram was adapted from R. NAPIERSKI (1987) by R.-U. GLÜCK.

a) setting (positioning) the cursor at one of the identification letters A, B or C, and
b) confirming this position by pressing < return >.
(As long as the < return >-key is not pressed, the computer   17
does not know whether your cursor setting is final.)

N1 = 'A'

   C1 You chose *Entering an answer.* The flashing cursor indicates
      that you have to press any < key > to continue.
      Sequence 1.

   C2 Sequence 1.

N2 = 'B'

   C1 You want to know more about the *function keys.* The flashing
      cursor asks you to press any < key > to continue.
      Sequence 2.

   C2 Sequence 2.

N3,1

      You are leaving this introduction! Press any < key > !

[1]   Entering with the Text Editor: *Entering an Answer.*

This is how to enter and edit (correct) your answers: 03
you can *delete* characters by pressing < **backspace** > and < **delete** >,
and you can *insert* text by < **insert** >. You can move the cursor
across the entering section to any position you want, using
the arrow keys.
You already know that you have to finish your answers by pressing
< return >, thus transmitting them to the computer.   09

Enter any sign ("behind" the cursor)!   12

N1,2 = b

   C1 Your answer will stay on the screen (if you do not react).
      If you wish to correct your answer, you do not have to delete
      it entirely: just leave on the screen what you want to keep and
      change where necessary.
      Edit your answer as you please.

   C2 You've had enough tries! Go back to the main menu.

I1

[2]   Learner Control: *Function Keys*

Key	Function	Description	05
<F1>	help window is called up	The help window appears on the screen. It explains the present procedure of entering an answer. The score is given where appropriate.	06
<F3>	repeat	Text, drawings and animations of the present theme are repeated.	10
<F5>	superscript	The single character *after* <F5> is printed above the line.	12
<F6>	subscript	The single character *after* <F6> is printed below the line.	14
<F9>	quit	The lesson is broken off. You may continue at the point where you broke off if you enter your name again.	16

<key>

---

1) Please press the key <F1> !   03
The help window appears in the middle of the screen.

2) Press the key <F3>: the previous text is   06
repeated.

Did you understand everything?   09

N1,1: 'y'
    Well done!
N2,1
    Never mind! You can repeat this unit as often as you like.

2. *Comments*

Learner control goes beyond what we have learnt about the representation of instruction so far.[1] The reason is that the learner's answers which control instruction are not *assessed*. This may lead to a point where answers become questions and comments become answers (given by the system). To achieve this kind of dialogue, the learner's possibilities to control instruction have to be pre-structured and defined precisely. In particular, potential operating mistakes have to be either ruled out or made subject of special consideration. Hence, problems concerning judging are only of a technical kind in learner control: it is only checked whether what the learner does is admissible or inadmissible. That is why the N-attribute occurs so often.

At the beginning of the present instrugram the learner is introduced to the operation of the instructional medium; he learns, e.g., how to enter something, or which keys have which meaning. In the main sequence the learner may select the subject matter ("entering an answer" or "the role of the function keys") or may finish the introduction. The related dialogue is structured in the following way: a short explanation is given after the first selection of a theme, leading on to the corresponding (sub-) sequence. If the learner wishes to work on the subsequences repeatedly, he is "branched" to them without getting a comment. As there are no high numbers for N1 and N2, the learner may go through the Sequences 1 and 2 as often as he likes before he leaves the hierarchy via N3. It is a characteristic feature of this kind of learner control (menu technique) that the learner himself determines the order in which he works on the lesson parts.

The key indicators printed in bold in Sequence 1 <**backspace**>, <**delete**> and <**insert**> represent key variables, or more precisely: variable key names. Each variable stands for a *particular* key function. The name of the function, however, depends on the respective *keyboard*. The English names, for example, may be replaced by German ones. (The meaning of the descriptive names in roman print like <arrow key> or <return> is obvious.) In the dialogue of this sequence, all practical input possibilities are covered by the answer requirement "N1 = b", where b stands for any basic[2] response. Inadmissible entries are not commented upon (I-*empty* comment). (As the corresponding keys are blocked, there can be no operational mistakes.)

Sequence 2 deals with the learner's possibilities of controlling the instructional flow. The corresponding reactions, prepared by the system and accessi-

---

[1] Learner control *stretches* but does not burst the frame of the description of instruction through Instruction Language.

[2] A response b is an element of the set B (see page 72).

ble via the function keys, may be called up by the learner only at times when learner activities are expected. Thus, rather than giving an answer, the learner may bring the theme of minimum instruction back to the screen by pressing the function key <F3>, he may call up help by pressing <F1> or may even break off the instruction by pressing <F9>.

Finally, the learner may get a general idea of the content of the lesson or of the hierarchies and sequences, or may go into the lesson at any point. (<F5> and <F6> have only a technical meaning: they enable the learner to write subscript and superscript characters for mathematical indices or powers.)

This disciplined freedom of control generates an elastic *learning environment*. The learner may use the freedom to do anything that suits his learning interest: look something up in a dictionary, make (real) experiments, watch a film, etc.

Bibliography

Alessi, S.M. & Trollip, S.R. *Computer-Based Instruction*. Englewood Cliffs, NJ: Prentice-Hall, 1985.

Ballreich,R. & Kuhlow, A. *Biomechanik der Sportarten* (Vol. 1). Stuttgart: Enke, 1986.

Becker, W. Zu: Eckel, Karl: Didaktiksprache, *Zeitschrift für Didaktik der Philosophie* 12 (1990), 113 - 114.

Beutel, F.K. Some Implications of Experimental Jurisprudence, *Harvard Law Review*, 48 (1934), 169 - 197.

Beutel, F.K. *Experimental Jurisprudence and the Scienstate*. Bielefeld: Gieseking, 1975.

Bork, A. Producing Computer Based Learning Material, *Journal of Computer-Based Instruction*, 11 (1984), 78 - 81.

Campbell, D.T. Reforms as Experiments, *American Psychologist* 24, (1969), 409 - 429.

Chargaff, E. Das Klappern der Experten, *Das Gymnasium in Rheinland-Pfalz*, Oct. (1984), 8 - 12.

Collis, B. *Computers, Curriculum and Whole-Class Instruction*. Belmont: Wadsworth, 1988.

Eckel, K. Vorschläge zur Abfassung von CUU-Didaktogrammen, *Grundlagenstudien aus Kybernetik und Geisteswissenschaften* 12 (1971), 93 - 99.

Eckel, K. Elemente einer Didaktiksprache, *Mitteilungen und Nachrichten des Deutschen Instituts für Internationale Pädagogische Forschung* 83/84 (1976), 8 - 32.

Eckel, K. Das Sozialexperiment — Finales Recht als Bindeglied zwischen Politik und Sozialwissenschaft, *Zeitschrift für Soziologie*, 7 (1978), 39 - 55.

Eckel, K. Grundbegriffe des Unterrichts — Die Grundstruktur des Unterrichtsablaufs, *Mitteilungen und Nachrichten des Deutschen Instituts für Internationale Pädagogische Forschung* 112/113 (1983), 74 - 95.

Eckel, K. Konventioneller und Objektivierter Unterricht, *fernmelde-praxis*, 63 (1986) 20, 777 - 787.

Eckel, K. *Didaktiksprache — Grundlagen einer strengen Unterrichtswissenschaft*. Köln & Wien: Böhlau, 1989.

Eckel, K. On the Stagnation in the Social Sciences and in Educational Research in Particular — Documentation, Causes, Remedies (unpublished report), Frankfurt am Main 1991.

Hay, J. G. *The Biomechanics of Sports Techniques*. Englewood Cliffs, NJ: Prentice-Hall, 1978.

Hillelsohn, J.M. Benchmarking Authoring Systems, *Journal of Computer-Based Instruction*, 11 (1984), 95 - 97.

Ihm, E. EPOS: Den Bildungsbedürfnissen in Europa begegnen. Ein DELTA-Projekt für die 'offenen Lernsysteme' der Zukunft, *EURO tele-bits*, ISSN 0941-6668, April (1992), 18 - 19.

Kearsley, G. Instructional Design and Authoring Software, *Journal of Instructional Development*, 7 (1984), 11 - 16.

Locatis, C.N. & Carr, V.H. Selecting Authoring Systems, *Journal of Computer-Based Instruction*, 12 (1985), 28 - 33.

Merrill, M.D. Where is the Authoring in Authoring Systems?, *Journal of Computer-Based Instruction*, 12 (1985), 90 - 96.

Merrill, M.D. Prescriptions for an Authoring System, *Journal of Computer-Based Instruction*, 14 (1987), 1 - 9.

Merrill, M. D. & Li, Z. An Instructional Design Expert System, *Journal of Computer-Based Instruction*, 16 (1989), 95 - 101.

Merrill, M. D., Li, Z. & Jones, M. K. Limitations of First Generation Instructional Design, *Educational Technology*, Jan. (1990), 7 - 11.

Merrill, M. D., Li, Z. & Jones, M. K. Second Generation Instructional Design, *Educational Technology*, Feb. (1990), 7 - 14.

Morrison, D.E. & Henkel, R.E. (Eds.) *The Significance Test Controversy*. Chicago: Aldine, 1970.

Napierski, R. Didaktogramm: Säuren und Basen, Wissenschaftliches Prüfungsamt der J.W. Goethe-Universität, Frankfurt a. M. 1987.

Palzer, E. Rezension. Eckel, K.: Didaktiksprache — Grundlagen einer strengen Unterrichtswissenschaft, *LOG IN*, 9 (1989), 76 - 77.

Popper, K.R. *The Open Society and its Enemies*. Princeton, NJ: Princeton University Press, 1950.

Popper, K.R. *The Logic of Scientific Discovery*. London: Hutchinson, 1959.

Popper, K.R. *The Poverty of Historicism*. London: Routledge and Kegan Paul, 1961.

Quine, W.V. *Mathematical Logic*. Cambridge, Mass.: Harvard University Press, 1951.

Schreiber, A. Entwicklung didaktischer Software auf Autorensystembasis, *Zentralblatt für Didaktik der Mathematik*, 22 (1990), 92 - 104.

Schreiber, A. Rezension. Eckel, K.: Didaktiksprache, *Zentralblatt für Didaktik der Mathematik*, 22 (1990), 114 - 116.

Sherwood, B.N. & Stone, D.E. Comments on Prescriptions for an Authoring System, *Journal of Computer-Based Instruction*, 14 (1987), 9 - 10.

Steinberg, F. R *Teaching Computers to Teach*. Hillsdale, NJ: Lawrence Erlbaum, 1984.

Weyl, H. *Philosophy of Mathematics and Natural Sciences*. Princeton, NJ: Princeton University Press, 1949.

List of Examples, Figures and Tables

179

180 Examples, Figures and Tables

Index

Two reference symbols are used in this index: the arrow referring to related terms and the asterisk. Asterisked words occur exclusively as subentries, with the corresponding page references appearing after the identical main entry. An example: having identified under the main entry 'answer' the asterisked entry '~ attribute' (answer attribute), the reader will find the corresponding page references after the main entry 'answer attribute' (together with a number of subentries).

E

F

G

H

J

K

L

M

T